"The missional church can often overlook the importance of eldership and governance. Hyatt and Briggs show us how vital these questions are in order for outward mission to be sustained. They provide a biblically rooted and mission-centered vision for eldership. The parts about the character, qualifications, and selection of elders were particularly helpful for me as a pastor."

Aaron Graham, lead pastor, The District Church

"The central theme of mission feels more paramount today than ever. Hyatt and Briggs have taken the indispensable biblical-cultural discussion of leadership beneath 'corporate strategies' and 'personality attraction' and have instead deep-rooted eldership in humble, courageous and contextualized co-missioning with the Master. This is a book for church influencers everywhere."

Tony Kriz, author of *Aloof: Figuring Out Life with a God Who Hides*, tonykriz.com

"The church has been in need of an updated understanding of eldership. With seasoned wisdom and theological rigor, Hyatt and Briggs team up to shift the role of elders from being a domesticated business board that focuses on maintenance, to a daring community of servant leaders who equip the whole church to join God's mission in the world. This is the best book I've read on eldership."

JR Woodward, national director, The V3 Movement; author of *Creating a Missional Culture*

"Hyatt and Briggs are like chiropractors for the church. They describe eldership as the church's 'bone structure,' which today is often in sore need of alignment and adjustment. They align the fundamental value of eldership by affirming its biblical purpose and the elders' commitment to God's mission in ordinary, everyday lives. Then they offer adjustments by unpacking in very practical and relevant ways what mission-minded elders look like, what derails them, how they create healthy culture, and then how elders manage the challenges that come, ultimately addressing the question of women elders. I found this book very helpful, and recommend it as an important resource for every church that wants a healthier, more active leadership structure."

MaryKate Morse, author, *Making Room for Leadership*, professor of leadership and spiritual formation, George Fox Evangelical Seminary

"If your church's eldership basically operates like the board of directors of a small religious enterprise, get them to read this book. Quick. J.R. Briggs and Bob Hyatt not only outline the biblical functions of eldership but they do so through the missional prism that the original biblical writers used. For them, eldership is missional insofar as elders are called to not only equip the church for mission but to eliminate as many factors as possible that could derail the missional orientation of the church. Biblical, practical, warm and inspiring."

Michael Frost, Morling College, Sydney; author of *The Road to Missional, Incarnate* and *Exiles*

"Intensely practical, thoroughly rich in wisdom, *Eldership and the Mission of God* is a book on church leadership that defies its stereotype. As well-honed practitioners and careful thinkers, Briggs and Hyatt recast everything about elder work for its call to mission. I wish I'd had this book twenty years ago."

David Fitch, Betty R. Lindner Chair of Evangelical Theology, Northern Seminary, author, *Prodigal Christianity*

ELDERSHIP
AND THE
MISSION
OF GOD

EQUIPPING TEAMS FOR
FAITHFUL CHURCH LEADERSHIP

J.R. BRIGGS & BOB HYATT

FOREWORD BY ALAN HIRSCH

IVP Books

An imprint of InterVarsity Press
Downers Grove, Illinois

InterVarsity Press
P.O. Box 1400, Downers Grove, IL 60515-1426
ivpress.com
email@ivpress.com

InterVarsity Press® is the book-publishing division of InterVarsity Christian Fellowship/USA®, a
movement of students and faculty active on campus at hundreds of universities, colleges and schools
of nursing in the United States of America, and a member movement of the International Fellowship
of Evangelical Students. For information about local and regional activities, visit intervarsity.org.

All Scripture quotations, unless otherwise indicated, are taken from the Holy Bible, New
International Version®. NIV®. Copyright ©1973, 1978, 1984 by International Bible Society. Used by
permission of Zondervan Publishing House. All rights reserved.

While all stories in this book are true, some names and identifying information may have been
changed to protect the privacy of individuals.

Published in association with the literary agency of Wolgemuth & Associates.

Cover design: David Fassett
Interior design: Beth McGill
Images: ©Milen Dobrev/iStockphoto

ISBN 978-0-8308-4118-9 (print)
ISBN 978-0-8308-9715-5 (digital)

Printed in the United States of America ♾

Library of Congress Cataloging-in-Publication Data

Briggs, J. R., 1979-
Eldership and the mission of God : equipping teams for faithful
church leadership / J.R. Briggs and Bob Hyatt ; foreword by Alan
Hirsch.
    pages cm
Includes bibliographical references.
ISBN 978-0-8308-4118-9 (pbk. : alk. paper)
1. Elders (Church officers) 2. Christian leadership. I. Title.
BV680.B75 2015
253--dc23
                                                            2014044443

P   20 19 18 17 16 15 14 13 12 11 10 9 8 7 6 5 4 3
Y   32 31 30 29 28 27 26 25 24 23 22 21 20 19 18

To the elders of The Renew Community and

The Evergreen Community.

Your leadership is worthy of double honor

(1 Timothy 5:17).

Contents

Foreword by Alan Hirsch 9

Introduction: Structured for Mission 13

1 Mission-Oriented Elders 21

2 Characteristics of Mission Alignment—
   and What Derails It 29

3 The Roles of an Elder. 39

4 Biblical Qualifications for an Elder. 55

5 Cultivating an Ethos Rooted in God's Mission 67

6 Selecting Elders. 81

7 Eldership as Spiritual Formation 97

8 Team Leadership 111

9 The Role of Elders in Decision Making 129

10 The Difficult Tasks of Elders. 143

11 What About Women Elders? 165

12 Practical Questions and Answers 179

Epilogue: Eldership as Stewardship. 193

Discussion Questions 195

Acknowledgments 204

Notes 206

Recommended Resources 212

About the Authors 215

Foreword

⫻

The church doesn't have a mission; God's mission has a church. And the calling of the church, first and foremost, is to seek God's rule and reign. As leaders called by God to lead in local Jesus communities, we cannot divorce mission from discipleship. Everything we do on mission must be saturated with the ethos of discipleship in the Way of Jesus. We will never be the movement Jesus imagined unless we first embrace and attempt to express discipleship in its authentic Jesus-imaging form. As Bonhoeffer shared so prophetically before the start of the Second World War, "a Christianity without discipleship is a Christianity without Christ."

That's why I am excited about this book. While this is a leadership book, it is much more of a "followership" book, teaching us to become kingdom agents who follow the founder of this movement of hope—and then in turn equipping, empowering and unleashing all of God's people within their unique callings. This is not a call for elders to embrace an inwardly focused fortress mentality, but rather to guide the church into the destiny that Jesus intended for it. This is what leaders—and specifically elders—in mission-focused contexts must strive after.

When it comes to church leadership, too much is simply assumed. Throughout his letters to the early churches of Asia Minor, the apostle Paul addresses issues that are crucial to becoming faithful, passionate and compassionate Jesus communities in new frontiers. But his instruction is not comprehensive: many issues are left unaddressed. There is, as the authors of this book state, significant freedom of form in God's community. While there are biblical guidelines given for our instruction for mission there is also a deep need for trust in and reliance upon the Holy Spirit as we seek to bless the world in Jesus' name.

J.R. and Bob give us something few—if any—books on church eldership have offered before: an accessible mission-directed primer on faithful leadership in localized, contextualized Jesus communities. Many have written on the topic through a biblical/ theological lens. This book certainly addresses these perspectives, but its real value in my opinion lies in the way it specifically addresses eldership through an *apostolic/missiological lens*. It takes the question seriously, "What has God called us to be and do in our current cultural context?" This focused view of contextually expressed biblical leadership is desperately needed in the North American church today. Thankfully, this book is not written from a theoretical ivory tower of generalities, but is rooted in on-the-ground experience, lived out in two very unique contexts.

Regardless of the size, age, geography, denomination or doctrinal conviction, every church is called to align with God's mission. My hope all along has been to help reawaken the suppressed apostolic imagination at the root of the Christian story and to encourage all of God's people to participate in it. Additionally, my hope is that this book will compel us to forego the prevalent version of decaffeinated Christianity and instead cultivate a missionary ethos that ignites faith communities to participate in the unrestrained and uncorked adventure of life with Jesus.

Alan Hirsch
Missiologist, speaker, founding director of Forge Network and author of The Forgotten Ways

Structured for Mission

◆

Writing a book about eldership is like talking about someone's bone structure. On the surface, it sounds uninteresting and slightly awkward. But imagine a human body without a skeletal structure. It would be unable to function appropriately, lacking the necessary shape, form and movement needed for human activity. It would also look incredibly unappealing.

When we meet people for the first time, we first notice their hair, eyes, smile and other body parts that help to facilitate social connection. Yet it is the skeletal structure that offers support that is vital to the health of the body. Undoubtedly, we would recognize a body without bones as seriously unhealthy.[1] Because church leaders are concerned about the health of the body of Christ, it is crucial to enter into a careful exploration of the skeletal structures of our churches.

When most people think about their faith communities, they immediately think about relationships or serving opportunities or preaching or worship. They think of stories and friendships and conversations with others—the relational receptors of the church. They don't often think about the structure of the church unless something is drastically wrong. When a church lacks structural health, that local body suffers, and there's no hiding it.

In his letters to New Testament churches, the apostle Paul spent a good deal of time and energy writing about structure. Often he started with the bone structure. When the bone structure of a local church was unhealthy, like a good physician, Paul addressed the situation, working carefully to correct it. Sometimes these churches were experiencing relational stress fractures, doctrinal bone breaks or ecclesial osteoporosis.

But Paul's work of setting the bones back into proper alignment wasn't to restructure for efficient management, security or personal comfort. His intent was to establish a healthy structure of relationships that enabled these communities to be uninhibited and unhindered in a focused, white-hot pursuit of God's mission. Paul wrote about the structure of local house churches striking the proper balance between giving enough instruction but not giving too much. And, as we'll explore, structure is important for mission, but overstructure can stifle it.

WHY A BOOK ON ELDERSHIP?

So why write a book about eldership—or more specifically, about eldership oriented around God's mission? Because it carries significant implications for becoming and remaining faithful witnesses in the world. If Paul spilled significant amounts of ink writing about mission-aligned leadership structures in the early formation of churches, why do we need more information about the role of elders today? Because few talk much about it, and it needs to be addressed.

Paul's groundwork on eldership is valuable and irreplaceable, but its context is critically important. Some elements of eldership are clear in Scripture, but many things are left unaddressed:

• What are elder's day-to-day or week-to-week responsibilities?

- How were elders selected—and how should we select them in our church?

- How long should elders serve?

- What did elder meetings look like, and what should they look like in our context?

Why does Paul leave these important details out of his writings? Because he wants each unique community to wrestle— by way of prayer and discussion—with what it means to faithfully bear witness to the gospel in a particular context.

That we must take up the task of embracing biblical eldership seriously is clear. Our responsibilities seem to be clear, but we need to prayerfully discern how they are embraced and expressed in our unique contexts. Just as human bodies operate on basic biological and physiological principles, churches operate on theological and missiological principles. And yet each body is unique, with its own strengths, pathologies, birthmarks, personality and distinct traits that set each of us apart and give us our uniqueness. Local churches are no different.

OUR CONTEXTS

I (J.R.) planted a church in the northern suburbs of Philadelphia in 2008. It's been incredibly difficult and yet filled with rewarding seasons of joy. A few dozen of us had a kingdom dream to see a community of faith focusing on Christ our King; we lived like an extended family, blessing the community to which we were sent.

Our launch was an exciting time, but because we had no official denominational home, we were anxious in our early formation, wondering how and what shape our new church would take. What were we to do? How were we to join with God in being a community centered on Jesus and sent into the world by the Spirit? And, very practically, where would we go for wise and practical help in our formation?

We knew wise decisions, appropriate expectations and a gospel ethos were crucial in our early stages. We knew Jesus-saturated leadership in a local church was (and is) paramount, and we knew we needed several wise, seasoned leaders to help us think through elements such as structure, oversight, theology, accountability, soul care and decision making. As a young leader and pastor serving on staff at two large churches prior to planting a church, I had never been invited to be a regular part of elder meetings. Now that I was planting a church, my anxiety grew as I realized I wanted to create a healthy elder culture in our church but had no experience to go on. I needed help.

I studied everything Paul said about eldership in his letters. I tried to read all I could on the formation and structure of church starts. I read any book I could find that dealt even remotely with the issue. I found and read resources on the roles of elders. I thought about churches that had healthy and unhealthy structures, and I wondered what we could learn from them. Where could I find wise leaders, seasoned pastors and battle-tested church planters who were willing and able to help our new church in this precious, formative and exciting season of ministry? Were there any resources that could help us navigate this significant early stage of the life of our church?

Bob (my friend and coauthor) helped to plant a church in 2004. The Evergreen Community meets at different times and in different locations across the city of Portland, Oregon, but its worship space—and indeed much of its community space—is in a pub. As a church that has found its niche in drawing people who have left church or written off the need for community, they have often struggled with an inherent distrust of leadership, and the leadership have found it necessary to explain—and, at times, reexplain—the need for elders and structure.

Before Evergreen, Bob's experience with elder teams had been almost uniformly negative. Meetings were filled with tension as various agendas—and occasionally factions—pushed back against each other, often with no concern for what God was saying and rarely with any desire to hear one another.

Although Bob and I pastor in different contexts and cultures, we have a shared conviction that elders of local churches are to be spiritual overseers, shepherds, teachers and equippers serving as consistent and God-honoring models of what a life with Christ looks like. We are convinced that pastors and elders are *not* to do all the work as the paid professionals of the church, but are called to equip God's people entrusted to them in their local congregations to fulfill their God-given role in his kingdom, operating as missionaries cleverly disguised as plumbers, teachers, stay-at-home parents, attorneys and the like.

Gratefully, the churches Bob and I help lead are members of a relational network of missional churches and church plants from around the country that seek to collaborate, train, equip, support and encourage one another on mission for the sake of the kingdom.[2] Bob and I met through this network. This is our tribe. Some of our closest friends are a part of this network; they have supported, encouraged and helped us in our development. With a diversity of background, size, history and context, the churches within our network share a vision to see healthy Jesus communities flourish.

By God's grace, we've been a part of churches that have healthy leaders. However, we also have seen unhealthy forms of eldership in local churches of all sizes, expressions and denominations. We've observed churches that seem to take business principles more seriously than biblical principles. We longed to find healthy models of eldership that were rooted in a biblical framework worked out in a missional context and provided healthy account-ability, expectation and structure—not to clone or copy, but to learn from and discern how that might look in our contexts.

Again, why did we write a book about eldership? Because when we were starting our churches, we looked high and low for resources on eldership within a missional church context but there was nothing available—at least nothing that seemed to fit what we sensed God was doing in our communities and what he was calling us into. This book is an attempt to create a resource that we wish had been available when we started our churches. And we are certain other pastors are longing for a similar resource.

HOW TO READ THIS BOOK

This book is not an exhaustive academic or theological treatise on biblical eldership. It is for church leaders and practitioners who want their faith communities to possess an ethos that is undeniably anchored in God's mission. Good books have been written on eldership that approach the topic from a theological perspective. This book, however, seeks to do something few—if any—have done before: explore eldership through a *missiological* lens and discuss its practical implications within local congregations. Certainly, a healthy and accurate missiological approach must include sound biblical theology, but exploring biblical eldership through the lens of God's mission in a local setting is essential to leading a church in pursuing God's heart. We want this book to address missiological postures and forms of eldership, but we hope it is practical for all leaders.

We do not want to give you simple answers or formulaic approaches to a contextualized topic. We attempt to offer forms without formulas, intentions free of equations. We've attempted to create a clear, compelling and accessible primer on eldership for churches that are taking their mission fields seriously.

We believe the local church is most healthy when it is pursuing God's heart and oriented around his mission. Mission-oriented leadership in a local church draws ecclesial form into incarnational functions.[3] When we participate in God's purposes together, we begin to see tangible glimpses of the heart of God in our ZIP codes.

Whether you're a pastor, a church planter, a seminary student, an elder, a leader in an unpaid vocational ministry role or otherwise, we hope this book equips you with tools and sharpens the tip of the arrow of your approach to mission-aligned leadership. We hope it helps you develop a skeletal structure that allows faithful partnership with God and his mission in naturally supernatural ways.

We will share stories to give you glimpses of how we have tried to serve and lead with a biblically faithful and mission-rooted approach to eldership. But let it be known that we are not encouraging anyone to copy what other churches are doing in their contexts, including ours. This is not a paint-by-number approach to church leadership. We need to learn how to take biblical principles and apply them in ways that allow God's people to discern God's voice together. This does not change the gospel story, nor does it lessen Scripture's place or effectiveness. If anything, it increases its significance.

Something Bigger Than the Status Quo

Paul wrote to the church in Ephesus, "Speaking the truth in love, we will in all things grow up into him who is the Head, that is, Christ. From him the whole body, joined and held together by every supporting ligament, grows and builds itself up in love, as each part does its work" (Ephesians 4:15-16). Having healthy elders does not guarantee a healthy church, but it does plant a local congregation in fertile soil.

We have a significant part to play, but of course we do not play the most important part. Christ is the head of his global church—

and of its various local expressions. God forbid that we ever believe we are the heroes of our churches. If we believe this, our congregations will never be capable of living up to their God-given identity nor will they bear faithful witness to the risen Christ. We look to him, the head, who in his immense grace invites us to wisely, faithfully and prayerfully depend on him in order to see a healthy faith community form—not for itself, but for the glory of God, who created the church in the first place.

1

Mission-Oriented Elders

*The separation of church from mission is theologically
indefensible. More and more Christians of the old churches
have come to recognize that a church that is not
"the church in mission" is no church at all.*

Lesslie Newbigin, *The Open Secret*

*And in him you too are being built together to become a
dwelling in which God lives by his Spirit.*

Paul, to the church in Ephesus

Floating Docks

My (J.R.'s) grandparents have owned a cabin on a lake in central Florida for almost forty years. Four generations of the Briggs family have spent precious time on this little piece of property nestled deep in the Ocala National Forest. Few things have changed on Owens Lake the past four decades, but the most significant change is the drop in water level. While it provides extra lakefront property at no extra charge, it poses a significant problem for many property owners.

While canoeing around the lake one afternoon with my son, I noticed dozens of docks that no longer touched the water's edge. Built years prior, when the water level was normal, they once connected land to water. Now none of these docks are fulfilling their functions. Though useful years ago, they are irrelevant today.

Our family cabin is one of the few properties on the lake that does not have a dock. On my canoe ride, I wondered if I were an owner with a useless dock on my property what I would do.

One option would be to extend the dock another fifteen or twenty feet out into the water. It would involve a great amount of time and money, but the dock would be useful once again.

Similarly, I could dig a narrow canal from the lake to the dock's edge. It would involve more backbreaking work without a sustainable, long-term solution; it would function until the water level changed again.

Another option would be to disassemble the dock and enjoy an unobstructed view. But I'm still left with the same reality: no functioning dock.

The simplest option would be to ignore the issue and leave the dock as is. That wouldn't solve the problem, but if I don't mind looking at it, who cares about the status quo?

But there was one more option I considered: I could build a floating dock. It's not as stable as a dock permanently attached to land, but no matter what the level of the water, it would never become obsolete. Ironically, on the entire lake, not a single property owner had a floating dock. Wouldn't it make a lot of sense to build that type of dock instead?

The North American church is experiencing an eerily similar dilemma. If the land is the mission of God, the water is culture and the docks are local churches, our purpose as elders is to work to connect and make accessible the mission of God with

the current culture. The stable churches that once met the ﹀
of connecting God's mission to the world with the cultu﹀
waters are now hardly touching the waters of today. Though the
docks haven't moved since they were built, the cultural water
levels have changed significantly. These docks may be stable and
impressive, but they are often useless and irrelevant.

Based on these conditions, it seems church leaders have
several options in leading local churches in the future:

- Add on to our already existing churches—new programs, styles,
  buildings or staff—which still runs the risk of being obsolete
  again in fifteen to twenty years as the cultural water levels
  change again.

- Ignore the issue altogether and let our churches continue on
  as they always have—further distancing our churches from
  participating in God's mission.

- Shut the doors of our churches—out of either convenience or
  necessity.

- Dig up the old way of doing church and build another one
  with a different model, approach or style. But then we risk
  becoming irrelevant when the water levels change again.

Or we can cultivate a mindset of adaptability by building
floating docks. These will lack the stability and predictability of
the old docks, and we run the risk of getting culturally wet. But
our churches can remain true to their purpose: *connecting the
mission of God to people, regardless of the cultural context.*

Elders are called to construct floating docks. This requires
unbelievable amounts of sacrifice—especially of our own personal preferences—but we must remain committed to God's
mission.

...ND Remaining on—Mission

...the topic of mission-aligned church lead-
...ant to define what we mean when we say
... *missional.* In my (J.R.'s) first day of class at seminary,
...y professor asked us a simple question: "How would you define ministry?" Despite many of us being in full-time vocational ministry, we had a difficult time coming up with an answer. Some gave long, drawn-out answers with impressive theological words and complex definitions that took even further explanation. When we had all shared our answers, our professor gave his definition: *meeting people where they are and journeying with them to where God wants them to be.*

I can still remember how this simple definition hit me. What struck me most was what ministry is *not.*

- Ministry is *not* waiting for people to come to us and *then* journeying with them to where God wants them to be. That's an old—and inaccurate—understanding.

- Ministry is *not* meeting people where they are and being content with where they are. That's friendship, not ministry.

- Ministry is *not* meeting people where they are and journeying with them to where *I* want them to be. That's not ministry, that's manipulation.

- Ministry is *not* meeting people where they are and journeying with them to where *they* want to be. That's Oprah with a little bit of Jesus sprinkled in.

Ministry is where we make ourselves accessible to others—*entering into their world on their terms*—with the hope that they encounter Christ. With this posture, there is a healthy burden and a *sentness.* But it is God who sets the agenda, trajectory and destination of people's lives and the pace at which people journey.

When we speak of churches led by mission-oriented elders, it means leaders take God's mission seriously; they seek to make it accessible, relatable and clear in the context in which God has sent them. Sentness is the belief that we are being sent or sending others, or both. In its truest sense, it's what we acknowledge when we pray the Lord's Prayer: Your kingdom come, your will be done, on earth as it is in heaven.

Often we miss the point, boiling the gospel down to a simple act of saying a prayer in order to ensure our eternal future. This is not the gospel. Scholar N. T. Wright said that if we make salvation about going to heaven, there is an awkward and embarrassing gap between our baptism and our funeral. When leaders grasp this sending orientation of God's Spirit, we realize we are not called to take earth to heaven when we die; instead, we are called to *bring heaven to earth as we live.* Leaders oriented around God's mission are rooted in being consistently present with others, are found in proximity to the people Jesus loves, are ready with a hope-filled proclamation of the story of God and maintain a committed involvement to meeting the needs of those around them, just as Jesus commanded his followers. To join faithfully with God's mission, elders must model this in local churches.

In many churches we've interacted with, we've noticed church leaders focusing an exorbitant amount of time, attention, energy, finances and conversation on the past and how it might inform the present. Too often, decisions are made based on precedent, security, sentimentality, history and tradition. Mission-driven elders are motivated less by preserving past structures and more by cultivating a healthy and faithful group of people that pursues the kingdom of God together. While tradition and history can develop kingdom leaders, make sure they never become sacred cows or idols.

UNDERSTANDING *MISSIO DEI*

Much has been talked about regarding *imago Dei* (the image of God) and *missio Dei* (the mission of God). These concepts are crucial to developing an accurate understanding of God that has implications on our identity and calling. Elders are called to cultivate a people that cares the most about the things that Jesus cared about. Sadly, some churches reflect either *missio die*—all talk, but no mission—or *missio me*—selfish ambition and self-centered pursuits veiled in spiritual language. This grieves the heart of the founder of our faith and the creator of the church.

Instead of "the image of God" and "the mission of God," a better translation of these two phrases might be the "imaging God" and the "missioning God"—a definition more rooted in God's character. The role of mission-oriented elders is to model a humanity that is broken yet redeemed and given incredible value (imago Dei) while reflecting the sending/sent heartbeat of a missioning God in the world (missio Dei). They see themselves not as preservers of tradition, but instead as shepherds of God's people, image bearers aligned with God's mission and culture cultivators within his kingdom. The call of elders in a local church context is to *faithfully lead God's people by imaging the character of a missioning God.*

Sending is built into the DNA of the triune God. The Father sends the Son and the Spirit. Jesus didn't merely show up; his Father sent him, and Jesus lived in confidence of his sentness. The Son sent the Spirit and the apostles. And the Spirit sends Jesus and the apostles.[1] If elders are seeking to display the character of God to a world in need, then we, too, will emanate the sending nature of the God we worship, the Jesus we follow and the Spirit we join.

In Acts, the "mother church" in Jerusalem experienced incredible growth, but it was not the only center of mission. Antioch became the mission center for the north and west. Additionally, the church in Philippi was the gateway to the spread of the gospel throughout Europe and the supporting center for Paul's missionary endeavors to the south.[2] These churches had a sending culture because they caught the heartbeat of our sending God.

GOD HAS A CHURCH FOR HIS MISSION

In his book *The Mission of God*, Christopher Wright wrote, "It is not so much the case that God has a mission for his church in the world but that God has a church for his mission in the world. Mission was not made for the church; the church was made for mission—God's mission."[3] We must remember that God has not called us to the sacred task of leadership to oversee a religious institution or a weekly spiritual event. Elders are called to shepherd a flock in pursuit of the heart of God, to seek the kingdom and to join faithfully in God's mission in a movement of discipleship that is both personal and corporate. If mission is to be pursued, elders must make a wholehearted commitment to leading differently.

Graham Buxton called ministry a dance with God. Local churches are invited to dance with the Spirit—to let him lead the dance, trust his embrace and let him teach us how to do it. We dance with God while joining hands with others and inviting them to dance with us.

2

Characteristics of Mission Alignment—and What Derails It

A church which pitches its tents without constantly looking out for new horizons, which does not continually strike camp, is being untrue to its calling. . . . We must play down our longing for certainty, accept what is risky, live by improvisation and experiment.

HANS KÜNG, *THE CHURCH*

Everything is fine, but the ship is still heading in the wrong direction.

EDWARD DE BONO

·⑾·

Elders who think like missionaries—in their jobs, families, neighborhoods, community responsibilities, schools—think like missionaries in their role in the church. They strive to see people exhibit a clear and compelling incarnational representation of

God to the world. Christopher Wright, in his helpful book *The Mission of God's People,* writes, "Churches, then, are to be communities around the world, planted, nurtured and connected through ministries of sending, going and supporting—for the sake of the name of Christ and the truth of the Gospel."[1]

Mission traction among a team of elders happens when the team is rooted and committed to the following elements.

AN EVER-DEEPENING DEPENDENCE ON PRAYER

It is nearly impossible to overemphasize how crucial prayer is to the pursuit of the mission of God. It is the fuel for mission. We may be able to minister for a season without it, but prayerless kingdom mission will not make a lasting impact. When Christ told his disciples they would be witnesses to the ends of the earth, their first response was to pray (Acts 1:12-14).

No doubt, one of the key factors to the growth of the early church was a commitment to prayer (Acts 2:42). It was also their immediate response to opposition and persecution (Acts 4:23-31; 12:12). As the church in Antioch was fueled by worship, prayer and fasting, the Spirit led them to initiate the first intentionally focused outreach outside of the Jewish people (Acts 13:1-3). Paul knew that radical faith, the power of the gospel and passionate prayer were a tremendous force in accomplishing God's mission.[2] The true test is this: does your time together as elders reveal a life that seeks the heart of God? Be a team committed to listening to God together. Prayer is the key ingredient to a unified elder team and to remaining on mission.

A KEEN SENSITIVITY TO HOW THE SPIRIT WORKS

When together we long for his Spirit to do more among his people, it is hard to believe God would not answer such a prayer. The calling of elders committed to God and his mission is not rooted primarily in charismatic leadership and efficient strategy, but in an active yet dependent pursuit of the Spirit together. The primary question of every elder team should be, *what is the Spirit's intent for our church?* And its efforts should be directed in responding in faith to that answer. We must be people who strive, as some have said, to eavesdrop on the Trinity.

A Commitment to Healthy, God-Honoring Relationships

God's mission is and will always be rooted in people, the focus of his love in the story of redemption. One of the significant metaphors for church in the New Testament is family. Are your elders modeling what it looks like to spend time with other members of God's family? Spending unrushed, quality time together is crucial to forming relational bonds of trust. Making time to be with other elders is crucial to a culture rooted in a context of trust and unity. How can people lead God's flock without knowing each other well?

A Passion for—and Commitment to—Discipleship

Discipleship and mission are inextricably linked. Before he left earth, Jesus charged his disciples to disciple all people (Matthew 28:18-20). There is a clear expectation that making disciples will be a part of the DNA of every follower of Jesus and every local church. Discipleship is the irreplaceable and lifelong task of becoming like Jesus by embodying his mission.[3] We once heard Dallas Willard say, "Imagine a church sign that reads, 'We teach all who seriously commit themselves to Jesus how to do everything He said to do.'"[4] Leaders rooted in God's mission don't merely talk about the importance of discipleship, *they bet the farm on it.* They measure the health of their churches by the quality of their disciples. Everything they do is rooted in a desire to see their people grow toward obedient Christlikeness in every area of their lives.

Neil Cole wrote these jolting words: "Ultimately each church will be evaluated by only one thing. Its disciples. Your church is only as good as its disciples. It does not matter how good your praise, preaching, programs or property are: if your disciples are passive, needy, consumerist, and not moving in the direction of radical obedience, your church is not good."[5] Mission-calibrated leadership measures the health and effectiveness of its church by the fruit of her disciples.

A PRIORITIZATION OF SENDING CAPACITY OVER SEATING CAPACITY

Elders rooted in mission care more about the question "How are we preparing, equipping and sending the people God has entrusted to us?" than "How was attendance last week?" When elders truly see the local church as a hub for shepherding, equipping and sending, they realize this impacts significant decisions regarding structure, metrics of success/health, budgeting, starting and ending key programs or events, and allotting time for staff and volunteers.

The goal is not that Christians come together to huddle and cuddle. They are being sent out, on mission, into the rest of their week—and they are helping to send others to do the same. This training helps each follower of Jesus within the church gain a posture of thinking and acting like humble and perceptive missionaries who are cleverly disguised as good neighbors, good employees and good friends.

UNITY WITHIN THE BODY

While prayer and God-honoring relationships are essential to mission-informed leadership, disagreements and conflict can arise. Unity does not mean uniformity. Unity within a church happens when, despite disagreement or difference, we are on the same page when it comes to the mission and philosophy of the church and its direction. It does not mean that the expressions of the church always line up perfectly with the convictions of all the elders, but that the elders are rooted in a deep understanding that what the church is doing is in alignment with God's heart.

Biblical community is not everyone getting along in every situation. In fact, biblical community is not the absence of conflict but the presence of Jesus in the midst of the conflict. Can we model Christlikeness to fellow elders in the midst of our differences?

RISK, CREATIVITY AND PERMISSION TO FAIL

While the nature and values of the gospel remain the same, their expression should always be changing. Stubbornness to change can lead to *methodolatry* and make the gospel inaccessible and undesirable to others. God and his mission are often full of surprises, so mission-focused leaders hold plans loosely and continue to ask what he desires.

We cannot respond with the seven deadly words of the church: "We've never done it that way before."[6] We must instead embrace a posture of "Whatever you want of us—and from us—God, we will do." One of the most significant and startling lessons we can learn from church history is that movements of renewal first happened on the fringe, not in the center of expected norms. Can we join him in those surprising places that force us to trust him with ever-deepening levels of faith?

Our role as elders is to seek God and ask him to stoke the coals of kingdom imagination in our own hearts and in the hearts of those in our congregation. Imagine if elders were the ones awakening hearts and minds of people with kingdom vision by saying things like "Imagine if we joined God by . . ." or "What if God called us as a church to . . ." or "I wonder if God is calling us to step out in the area of . . ." When guided by the Spirit and rooted in wisdom, this type of kingdom-initiated vision is contagious.

But imagination involves risk and courage, which requires permission to fail—and grace when it happens. If we are afraid of failure, our churches will never pursue new outposts for reaching new people within various cultures and contexts. To be elders committed to expressing God's mission is to lead with courage as we pursue a mission larger than ourselves.

As Alan Hirsch and Michael Frost wrote,

> Missional leadership is courageous and willing to try new things and risk all if necessary to see the kingdom come. Every church should have a Research and Development department; that is, a forum for dreaming, where nothing is impossible and no thought too outrageous. And every authentic missional church will experiment like mad in order to find new and accessible ways of doing and being the people of God.[7]

This requires great courage from the leaders of local congregations, but it's amazing what God does with such risky faith. Imagine what God might do if every local church saw itself as a research and development laboratory for the kingdom of God.

EVIDENT WISDOM

Courage and risk are necessary, but so is wisdom. Wisdom without courage is risk-less, and courage without wisdom is reckless, but wisdom and courage together are priceless. It is essential to maintain an equal emphasis on roots (being grounded and disciplined posture) and wings (taking risks and taking flight) for the sake of the kingdom.

A collective, proactive pursuit of wisdom among elders honors the Lord. It's nearly impossible to honor God when elders are acting unwisely. The book of Proverbs repeatedly communicates the preciousness of wisdom. James tells us that if we lack wisdom, we are to ask God, who gives generously and faultlessly. The promise given to us is that when we ask, he will provide it for us (James 1:5). Elders, therefore, should be asking the Lord frequently for wisdom—both for general oversight and for unique situations that arise.

WHAT DERAILS MISSION?

While there are key factors in mission alignment, several elements can derail mission in churches. Here are seven significant elements to avoid.

1. Pride, unconfessed sin and spiritual immaturity. Few things bring a church down more significantly than spiritually immature elders who are prideful, stubborn, self-seeking, conceited and/or agenda driven. Such things erode trust and unity—two elements essential for leading God's people effectively. Elders who are faithful, pliable, humble and accessible to the Spirit, who are open to correction and who have teachable spirits are needed.

2. Fear of the unknown and/or of ramifications of difficult decisions. Sadly, many decisions made by elder teams are rooted more in fear than in pursuing God's mission. If we aren't careful, issues can be wrapped in spiritual language but are disguised as fear. There might not be enough money or volunteers or attendees or momentum or capable leaders or programs to keep up with the church down the street. Sadly, we can be tempted to make decisions driven by maintenance rather than mission, leading to a domesticated expression of our wild and adventurous God.

3. Focusing too much time and energy on intramural issues. Many jokes are made about how churches split over the color of the carpet, but matters even more trivial have caused problems and stalled mission. These issues may not split the church, but they distract us from the most significant matters when we focus large amounts of time, energy and discussion on them. It is all too easy to get caught up in the minutiae of ministry and miss the big picture. Spend time on what matters most: the people and causes close to the heart of God. When we fail to do so, those inside the church remain content while those outside the church continue to believe the church offers nothing to them.

4. A deep-seated spirit of suspicion or distrust. If there is resentment, unresolved tension, bitterness, grudge holding or a lack of trust among the leaders, there will be damaging ramifications in the culture of the church. Churches are longing to see their leaders trust God and each other more deeply. If elders can't model biblical community within their team, why would we expect to see biblical community among the rest of the congregation? We must model forgiveness and reconciliation—where the fullness of grace meets the fullness of truth in redemptive relationships among elders.

5. Comfort and self-preservation. Neil Cole wrote that the greatest sin of the North American church is self-preservation.[8] One of the single greatest barriers to mission-aligned churches is the inertia of tradition. In John 12, Jesus says that unless a seed falls to the ground and dies, it will not produce fruit. His call on our lives is that we die to ourselves and find our lives hidden in him. It is natural for people and churches in a consumer-saturated North American context to gravitate toward comfort and ease, sometimes even without realizing it. Wise elders are keenly aware of this subtle yet dangerous temptation to lean toward personal comfort.

6. Wrongly defined metrics of success (or succeeding in all the wrong things). How we define success will define our churches. Many churches import success metrics from the corporate world, thus missing the point of God's heart for the church.

The primary concern of the elders should be spiritual health, not numeric metrics. Here are some questions elders might ask:

- What does Scripture say that Jesus valued—and is that what our church values most?

- Should we measure our success in numbers and growth based on building size, attendance and the state of the budget—or are there other measurements that match more closely with the values of the kingdom?

- What is Christ calling us into?

- Where are we striving for control, comfort and convenience— and what might we have to sacrifice in order to join closely with his heart?

7. The prioritization of pragmatism. An overemphasis on what works can significantly hinder a church from pursuing God's heart in new frontiers. Wisdom is an essential element of leading faithfully, but often so-called "wisdom" can be a veiled excuse to do what is safe, what is known and what has always been done in the past. Being wise and practical can be a gift, but raising the priority of pragmatism to an unhealthy level can cause a church to go inward, look backward and reflect on its glory days rather than pursue God's glory into the future.

3

The Roles of an Elder

We do not find Paul concerning himself with the size
of the churches or with questions about their growth.
His primary concern is with their faithfulness,
with the integrity of their witness.

LESSLIE NEWBIGIN, *THE OPEN SECRET*

If serving someone is beneath you,
then leadership is above you.

MIKE PILAVACHI

᠅

What are the primary roles and responsibilities of an elder—
and where did you develop your understanding of them?" We've
asked numerous pastors, elders and congregants this question,
and we usually hear three primary answers.

- *From what they observe.* What the elders at their current church
  model to them—whether healthy or unhealthy—is what they

inherit as their understanding. How elders interact up front in a service or in the hallways before or after services communicate what they should do.

* *A culturally inherited understanding of what was modeled to them when they were growing up.* Often the unspoken cultural expectations and assumptions of elders left the largest impression.

* *Inherited denominational structures.* Most denominations have well-established elder structures in their polity. Some articulate their denomination's approach to eldership.

Of the answers we received, few conveyed a coherent and well-developed framework for the roles and responsibilities of an elder from the Scriptures themselves.

THE POSTURE OF AN ELDER

Before we get into the functions of an elder, it is important that we start with the posture of an elder. A church does not belong to the elders, the pastor or even the members of the congregation. The church belongs to Christ. That must burn in our hearts if we are to accept the biblical teachings regarding church order and life.[1] If elders flaunt their authority or power, it can be destructive, but if the posture of elders is one of servanthood, exemplifying Christ's posture found in Philippians 2, it is a beautiful model for the larger church.

One of the most important ways our (J.R.'s) elders have attempted to cultivate a spirit that "nothing is below us" is to make sure we are serving—along with our spouses—with the babies and children during our worship gatherings. We have the deep conviction that we have a role to serve not just the adults but also the children of the church. Sometimes during worship, I duck out from our gathering and peek in our children's ministry classrooms. What I sometimes find is an elder on all fours, playing a silly game with a toddler or patiently rocking a screaming infant or helping a child finish a craft or teaching hand motions to a song. As I watch them, I can't help but smile; our children—and our parents—are learning that our elders can be trusted and that they are here to serve the church in whatever capacity is needed. They are modeling servanthood to the next generation, but it also keeps our own hearts in check, reminding us that nothing is below us. If we as elders refuse to lower ourselves to even the "ordinary" tasks, we have forgotten our calling to be like Jesus.

THE FIVE PRIMARY FUNCTIONS OF AN ELDER

The word *elder* is the most commonly used term for a leader in the New Testament, while the word *pastor* occurs only once in the New Testament (Ephesians 4:11-13).[2] The first mention of Christian elders is in Acts, when the church in Antioch sent Barnabas and Paul to the Jerusalem elders with money to aid in famine relief (Acts 11:30).

The term *elder* is used 180 times in the Old Testament and refers either to a person of old age or a leader of a community designated to make decisions or perform official functions. About two thirds of the uses of the term refer to respected community leaders.[3] They were representative of a larger group of people, and they usually became elders because of their moral authority; they were decision makers for a particular group of people. Today many scholars believe that the origin of the New Testament elder is the Jewish synagogue elder.

In a modern context, elders carry a level of influence based not on title but on moral consistency, integrity and trust. They are oriented in and on God's mission, and they are rooted in making decisions on behalf of the community that guide a group of people closer to God's heart.

There are five primary biblical functions of an elder.

1. Overseer. On several occasions, Paul writes that the role of an elder is to oversee a particular congregation. In fact, elders and overseers are two titles used interchangeably throughout the New Testament. When Paul wrote to Timothy (1 Timothy 3:1-2; 5:17-20) and to Titus in Crete (Titus 1:5-7), he used both terms— as did Peter (1 Peter 5:1-2).[4]

Two Greek words are often used to describe an elder/overseer in the New Testament. Though closely related, they have slight differences. *Episkopos* (where we get the word *episcopal*) means "overseer" or "guardian" and often refers to the role of bishop. *Presbuteros* (where we get the word *presbytery*) means "elder" or "priest" and often refers to priests or elders in a congregation (both staff and nonstaff).[5] This is not a domineering, power-wielding position. Overseers are not overlords; they are servants in their role of supervision and oversight of an entire congregation entrusted to their care by God to steward appropriately.

There are two main forms of oversight. The primary role is spiritual oversight, which includes watching over God's flock. This includes protection, guidance, instruction and presence among the people God has called them to serve. Spiritual oversight is evidenced through a marked commitment to prayer and intercession for and with the congregation, providing church discipline when necessary, clarifying doctrinal stances and cultivating God's mission. It also includes oversight of each other as elders. The book of Acts gives instructions to leaders, saying, "Keep watch over yourselves and all the flock of which the Holy Spirit has made you overseers" (Acts 20:28).

In addition to spiritual oversight, elders are called to organizational oversight. Not merely a spiritual and relational presence, an elder also provides systems that support the overall life of the church. This may include making wise, God-honoring decisions regarding budgets, personnel and facilities. Though these decisions may seem "unspiritual" and at times trivial, they can be incredibly important and strategic in the overall vision of the church. Several New Testament writers tell us that one of the roles of an elder is to manage (*proistemi*) (for example, in 1 Thessalonians 5:12). However, a proper balance between spiritual and organizational oversight is crucial to healthy leadership. Too much business driven by an elder meeting agenda can lead to too little spiritual discernment saturated in prayer. An overemphasis on management can lead to a church soft on mission and hard on business.

Finding a proper balance is essential for the health of any team of elders. But it is crucial that elders realize that their primary responsibility of oversight is spiritual. Certainly building maintenance, budget projections and hiring decisions are important—and they can and should be seen as spiritual in nature—but these cannot become a higher priority than loving, praying, serving, communicating the Scriptures clearly and shepherding the church into greater spiritual depth with Christ. Both spiritual and organizational oversight are essential, but they should lead the congregation toward a deeper commitment to the Father's heart.

2. Shepherd. Shepherding God's flock is not a résumé-boosting role; it means lowering ourselves to be among a group of messy people. To shepherd we must be with the sheep entrusted to us and to care for their well-being (Jeremiah 3:15). The work of a shepherd is not self-glorifying nor should it be done for fame or to acquire power, status or privilege. Christ is the Good Shepherd, and we are his undershepherds, looking to him for direction with the flock he has entrusted to our care on his behalf.[6] Availability and accessibility are crucial to fulfilling our role as shepherds faithfully.

Shepherds lead, and their leadership must be indelibly marked by love. Paul's second letter to the Corinthian church details the sin and immaturity of a newly formed church. Even though the immaturity and messiness of these people frustrate Paul, he admits how much he loves them and cares about them. Shepherding God's flock can be inefficient. In fact, pastoral work and efficiency do not go well together.

Refusing to be involved in people's lives has a dangerous side: the less we truly know the people entrusted to our care, the easier it is to treat them like a commodity. People don't like to be used in order for leaders to accomplish their big dreams and exciting plans. It can feel dehumanizing. The church is rooted in relationships. The higher the value we place on relationships, the less we are tempted to use people for our own means. We love people; we don't use people.

Shepherds provide protection for the flock (Acts 20:29). Their job is not just to make sure doctrine is sound, but also to confront those who stand against truth (Titus 1:9). Sometimes their role is to protect the sheep from predators; other times it is to protect the sheep from themselves, guarding them from what they want, knowing it would do more harm than good. Ezekiel shares God's harsh message for the shepherds of Israel who abused their position of leadership, and it would be wise for us to take warning as spiritual shepherds:

> Son of man, prophesy against the shepherds of Israel; prophesy and say to them: "This is what the Sovereign Lord says: Woe to the shepherds of Israel who only take care of themselves! Should not shepherds take care of the flock? You eat the curds, clothe yourselves with the wool and slaughter the choice animals, but you do not take care of the flock. You have not strengthened the weak or healed the sick or bound up the injured. You have not brought back the strays or searched for the lost. You have ruled them harshly and brutally." (Ezekiel 34:2-4)

In essence, elders who fulfill their role as shepherds see themselves as spiritual parents to those entrusted to their care.

One of the most significant ways elders shepherd a local congregation is through intercessory prayer. This involves a life marked by personal prayer, regular time in prayer among elders and time spent praying with people within the church. One of our elders, Tim, understands how crucial prayer is for our church. He continually pushes our elders into deeper levels and times of prayer in our meetings. For the past few years, he and his wife, Cindy, have led a weekly time of prayer to which they invite everyone from our church. Every Tuesday night, their home is open to pray, and groups gather to seek God's heart and lift up hurting people from our church body.

Tim and Cindy lead in other ways as well. They host many of our elder meetings; they regularly open their home to others for dinner; and numerous young couples seek out their wisdom. Cindy mentors other young women. They help lead Communion and times of prayer when our church gathers. They shepherd others by generously giving out warm hugs and embraces to just about everyone they encounter. People know, beyond a shadow of a doubt, that they love Jesus, they love each other, they love people, and they love seeing people step into the fullness of God's heart. They are not seminary trained. Tim is a virologist for a pharmaceutical company, and Cindy works as a part-time landscape architect. But their lack of formal training does not limit their ability to love others.

3. Teacher. Paul writes that one of the roles of an elder is to teach (1 Timothy 5:17). Teaching can take place in various settings and expressions, both formal and informal. It can occur from the pulpit or in a living room, in a Sunday school room or over coffee. Most importantly, an elder's *life* must teach, communicating clearly what it means to follow Jesus. To teach well, elders must have a hunger for the Scriptures and crave to know the heart of God more. They also need a teachable spirit, a hunger to remain at the feet of the master teacher, Jesus.

How else do elders teach? They must be sufficiently trained and gifted to handle the word of truth accurately (2 Timothy 2:15) and to help people contend for the faith (Jude 3). Elders give instruction in sound doctrine, including refuting those who contradict it (Titus 1:9). Without a firm grounding, truth can be eroded.

Elders also teach people in wise living. Our elders have taught individuals, couples and families how to handle their personal finances in a godly way, led premarital counseling sessions, offered wise instruction on how to live for Christ in the workplace and trained others in how to engage the culture as a Christian with a missionary posture. All of these are valuable areas of spiritual growth that help build up the body to full maturity.

4. Equipper. Busyness does not equate to mission. Simply because a group of God's people is active in a local church doesn't mean there is traction in its participation in God's mission. Many churches we've interacted with operate as spiritual treadmills that involve much activity but no real movement. Many things—even good things—can occur in the life of a church on a regular basis, but if equipping is not happening, we must question the health of the congregation. Ephesians roots us in our identity found in Christ, but it is also a great book for understanding the importance of equipping God's people for works of service (Ephesians 2:8-10; 4:11-13).

A few years ago, our church spent the summer months soaking in the waters of Ephesians, and the teaching was handled entirely by our elders. As a team, we wanted everyone in our church to know who they are in Christ and to understand what role we all play in God's story. In the midst of the teaching, we communicated regularly that the elders' job was not to do ministry for them, but to equip the entire church so every one of us lives out of our gifts and passions in order to participate in God's work in the world (Luke 10:2). We believe this is what Paul meant when he wrote, "Try to excel in gifts that build up the church" (1 Corinthians 14:12).

In the ancient times, equipping had four different meanings: setting a broken bone correctly, packing a ship with supplies for a long journey, restoring something to its original condition and preparing a soldier for battle. When leaders in the church begin to take seriously the call of equipping in their congregations, they begin to address the issues of brokenness and healing in the world, they prepare others for the journey, and they help restore people to their original condition of shalom. They don't just give people the truth; they also help them find ways to be strengthened for the battle ahead.

Elders cannot think of themselves as experts or as mere dispensers of information; instead, they must see themselves as God-commissioned equippers of others.

It is nearly impossible for one primary leader to guide an entire congregation—regardless of its size—into mission-saturated impulses and God-honoring fruit. This is why it must be done by and with others, starting with elders. Our leaders talk regularly about making sure we pass the School Bus Test: if the pastors of our church were hit by a school bus and died, what would happen to our church? This may sound morbid, but it is important.

If we take equipping seriously, we know that our job is to work ourselves out of a job. If our calling is to equip others and to see them grow up into maturity, we hope and pray that we've set up our church well—our elders, our leadership community and our entire congregation—to provide a natural path to step in and step up in leadership after we are gone. School Bus Test discussions keep us humble, reminding us that healthy churches are not built entirely around one or two key leaders. In addition, they constantly hold our feet to the fire to ensure we are devoted to training and equipping other leaders in the Way of Jesus.

It is important that we make a clear distinction here: equipping and delegation are two different things. Delegation is when someone in authority passes off tasks to others and expects them to do those tasks in a certain way. Equipping is much different. To equip is to give others permission to pursue a stated mission; it is to grant authority to engage and to do things in a way that they believe is most effective. To equip effectively is to empower, train, unleash and release others—even if they do things differently than we would. When we think like equippers, we begin to think more in terms of multiplication rather than addition. A refusal to take equipping seriously can stunt the growth and spiritual maturity of those we are leading. If elders do ministry by themselves, they are simply thinking via addition, but when elders build up the body through equipping, they are empowering and unleashing others into their God-given giftings, passions and wirings.

5. Example. We are called to be "examples to the flock" (1 Peter 5:3). The author of Hebrews writes, "Remember your leaders, who spoke the word of God to you. Consider the outcome of their way of life and imitate their faith" (Hebrews 13:7). How can this occur if it is not modeled well? Providing a consistent example for others to see is one of the primary ways elders can lead in their context. People are watching closely to see if the leaders of a local church are exhibiting in their homes, neighborhoods and places of work what they see in the sanctuary.

Elders may provide wise oversight, show skill in teaching, shepherd others and equip others to live out their callings, but if their lives are inconsistent or their characters immature, they will be perceived as hollow and hypocritical and will fail to build trust among the people entrusted to their care.

Because more is caught than taught, one of the greatest ways to communicate to believers who are immature and struggling in their faith is to expose them to godly examples.[7] When Peter wrote to leaders, instructing them to be examples to the flock, the word *example* is often translated as *pattern*. The implication is *consistency of faith and goodness*. Good leadership—whether in the corporate world, the military, a nonprofit organization, an elementary school or a church—is built on trust. It's why character is so crucial to the biblical qualifications laid out in the New Testament. When good character is absent, so is moral and spiritual influence.

Paul wrote, "Follow my example, as I follow the example of Christ" (1 Corinthians 11:1). He wasn't arrogant; he was confident that his life lived with Christ was worthy of imitation. Ministry flows out of being. In other words, we cannot export what we have not first imported.[8]

When elders live out their biblical calling faithfully, they provide oversight (both spiritually and organizationally), shepherd people in their needs, teach in various settings and expressions, equip the body to participate with God and his mission and give a clear examples of what a life with Christ looks like—not as perfect examples, but as pointers to Christ.

What Mission-Shaped Elders Are Not

In order to understand the role of elders, it is important to understand what an elder is not. Tragically, many elders are chosen for all the wrong reasons and thus create a leadership structure inconsistent with the Scriptures.

1. Mission-shaped elders do not assume the posture of a board of directors. While the IRS requires any church or nonprofit organization to have a board of directors to receive the benefit of a tax-exempt status, it is important to make a clear distinction between the spiritual role of elders and the legal requirements of a board of directors.

Of course, operating within the guidelines of the government is important for the integrity and legal standing of the church. Failure to do so can lead to the revocation of tax-exempt status or further legal action. However, it is important to realize the distinct difference between a board of directors (governmentally defined) and a team of elders (scripturally defined). Making sure the church knows its leaders are proactively seeking to value people and not merely operating as a corporate entity is essential in remaining on mission with Christ. (More on the selection of elders in chapter 6.) *Elder* should not be a code word for "board member" but instead should represent a godly, spiritually mature follower of Jesus.

2. Mission-shaped elders do not lead to be popular or to possess power. Many elders are chosen because of their popularity, because of their influence in the church or community or because their family is established or well connected. Family power struggles affect churches significantly. Though these struggles may not be on the surface, they can linger underground and affect decision making in subtle—or obvious—ways. If the posture of an elder or potential elder is one of grabbing power, that must be dealt with immediately.

Elders with humble hearts make a commitment in their role to God, to each other and to the people they are called to serve that nothing is below them. They are willing to give up all rights and personal preferences, if needed, to serve Christ and the pursuit of God's mission in a local context.

3. Mission-shaped elders are not appointed primarily because they are wealthy. The sad fact remains—and it cannot be ignored—that, for many churches in North America, money becomes an important factor in the consideration and/or selection of elders. Pastors and other elders, concerned with maintaining a balanced budget, often choose people with money, believing that as they make the key decisions in the church, they can depend on their gifts. This is a practice taken right out of the business world that relies more on finances than on character.

4. *Mission-shaped elders do not have a laissez-faire mentality.* Many elders serve in an oversight role that remains relationally distanced from the community they oversee. Some elder teams meet once a quarter to go over finances, the senior pastor's concerns, hiring and other decisions. This is important, but so is encouraging people in their spiritual journey, challenging sin, teaching the Scriptures, mobilizing others into mission and engaging in regular and committed prayer and intercession on behalf of the people in the congregation. This cannot happen from a distance; it must be up close.

Yes, elders have jobs, families and outside responsibilities for which they are responsible. Those responsibilities should not be neglected, of course. There is, however, an element of sacrifice and an ownership of the vision of the church and its relationships. Elders oriented around mission need to model to the congregation what it means to be all in. Many charismatic and strong-willed pastors have worked hard to create a team of elders who operate as yes men or yes women, so they can easily get their ideas or agendas pushed through for approval. Power plays and subtle manipulation are at work in these unhealthy cultures. Though it may never be verbalized, the elders are usually aware of this manipulation.

Though theoretically the church is elder led, in reality much of the time it is senior pastor led. When almost all the authority and power are given to one person, many issues can surface, not the least of which is in the heart of the senior pastor. This lack of accountability can lead to destructive results; we've witnessed firsthand that this can leave entire congregations hurting. Courageous elders who proactively seek the truth are needed, even if it means offering pushback to the lead pastor. Elders are not to be conflict avoiders, but to be pursuers of truth. Pursuing the truth sometimes brings about awkwardness and vulnerability, but also amazing moments of healthy community.

5. Mission-shaped elders are not primarily disciplinarians. While church discipline certainly is a significant role of an elder (spiritual oversight), elders who posture themselves as the chief disciplinarians find they cultivate (knowingly and unknowingly) a culture of fear in the congregation. Suspicion and worry should not be what people experience when elders are around, but it is easy to feel this way when elders posture themselves as morality police. If shepherds deeply and sincerely love their sheep, fear is not the dominating emotion among them. Sometimes suspicion and fear among congregants is well founded, as some elders lead only when a conflict arises or church discipline seems necessary.

Conversely, mission-shaped elders have the courage to deal with problems, conflicts and sinful situations head-on. They do not shy away from pursuing truth in circumstances, even if it is difficult or potentially awkward. Elders cannot tolerate sin, untruthful and harmful thinking, or unwise living in the people they are called to oversee. We cannot obediently pursue God's mission if we blatantly ignore the things God clearly commands we obey.

MODELING FOR THE COMMUNITY

We cannot stress enough the vital importance of leaders modeling a healthy life with God amid the people in the local church. Living coherent lives obedient to Jesus in word and deed is crucial for faithful, God-honoring leadership. We can think of no better way for things to be caught rather than taught than in a local church settings and through the prayer and leadership of elders. People learn to pray by experiencing prayer with others and by trying it themselves. People learn about leadership in a local church setting by what they see modeled by other leaders in the congregation, especially the pastors and elders.

An elder team should be a microcosm of the larger organism of the church. *It is a community within a community.* A team of elders has to model what it desires its church to become. We have never heard of a healthy church that had a chronically unhealthy and damaging team of elders. Pastors and elders within a local church context have the sacred and significant responsibility of cultivating a culture that cares the most about the things that Jesus cared the most about. This starts with the local church's leaders themselves.

Biblical Qualifications for an Elder

Whoever aspires to be an overseer desires a noble task.

A good character is the best tombstone. Those who loved you and were helped by you will remember you when forget-me-nots have withered. Carve your name on hearts, not on marble.

CHARLES SPURGEON

᭢᭢᭢

THE IMPORTANCE OF CHARACTER

Scripture doesn't offer an exact and specific way to structure a local church, but it does offer specific elements of the character of church leaders. While writing to churches in Asia Minor, Paul spelled out specific qualifications for elders of local congregations. He wanted local churches to realize that *who elders are* (their character) is more important than *what elders do* (the specific roles and responsibilities they perform). What people do flows out of who they are. The roots inform the fruits.

The root of the word *integrity* is *integer*—a whole number. When someone is full of integrity, he or she is the same person all the way through. The evil one places many distractions and threats in the path of people and churches. The last thing a church needs is to have elders who derail direction and unity, and distract the church's focus from the mission of God and the pursuit of his kingdom. The spiritual maturity and godly character of each individual elder has massive implications for the unity and maturity of the entire team.

When Paul wrote these specific qualifications, his *missiological purpose* was about embodying a life with Christ that was twofold: first, modeling what a life with Christ looks like, remembering that more is caught than taught, and second, eliminating as many factors as possible that could derail the mission orientation within a local church.

Churches may view elders as the white blood cells of a local church body, fighting off infection and restoring health. This certainly is part of it, but not all. They are also the red blood cells, carrying oxygen to other cells. Elders are called to function as both white and red blood cells, seeing the local church remain healthy and functioning as Jesus intended.

Simply put, the elders should be the best people in your church. By best, we do not mean the most influential, the most loyal, the wealthiest, the longest-attending members or the most powerful inside or outside the church. They should be the most spiritually mature.

One Sunday morning, when our (J.R.'s) elders announced to our church the name of a potential elder we were prayerfully considering, we could sense an affirmation in the room during the announcement. Afterward, someone approached me and said, "Truthfully, he has been operating in the role of an elder already—

he just hasn't been given the title yet." This person's life and leadership had already been clearly exhibited within the church, and most had deep respect for him already. People respected his way of life and felt cared for. Ultimately, elders must have a healthy, faithful relationship with God that has been evidenced over a long time in the context of a community. Their lives are not perfect, but they clearly point people in the direction of Christ.

ELDER QUALIFICATIONS

Specific elder qualifications are laid out in 1 Timothy 3:1-7 and Titus 1:5-9. There are fifteen qualifications in each passage, though slightly different characteristics in each list. There are positive characteristics to emulate and negative characteristics to avoid. These qualifications fall into three distinct categories: situational, family and moral.[1]

1. Situational qualifications.

A desire to serve (1 Timothy 3:1). A posture of readiness and eagerness is contagious in any setting—including the noble task of spiritual overseeing. Simply because someone is qualified to serve due to godly character does not mean he feels called or desires to serve in such a role. Sometimes there are outside factors and underlying forces—big and small, good and bad—that a affect a person's desire to be involved. Elders who serve halfheartedly or begrudgingly do a disservice to the local body of Christ.

One key question an existing elder team can ask a potential elder is "Are you willing and able to serve as an elder in our church?" I (J.R.) remember one potential elder we approached who was willing, but because he had to travel out of state three to four times a month for business, he did not believe he could fulfill the role faithfully and would be neglecting the leadership of his family at home. He respectfully declined in order to serve faithfully in these other areas of responsibility. Though he was wise and well respected for his faith, and our church would have benefited from his leadership as an elder, he made a wise decision.

Able to teach (1 Timothy 3:2; Titus 1:9). As addressed earlier, the role of teaching is a core element of an elder. Writing to the Cretan leaders, Paul said an elder must "hold firm to the trustworthy word as taught, so that he may be able to give instruction in sound doctrine and also to rebuke those who contradict it" (Titus 1:9 ESV). This does not mean elders must preach regularly when the church gathers, but it does mean they take instructing and guiding people to maturity in Christ seriously. At times, the *informal* teaching that exists among elders within a congregation can be more significant for the health of the church than formal instruction or preaching.

Not a recent convert (1 Timothy 3:6). Paul gives a reason for not installing a new believer into leadership: because he may be puffed up with conceit and fall into condemnation of the devil (1 Timothy 3:6). We must avoid making hasty decisions and elevating new Christians to levels of influence too quickly. They need to be built into and discipled; throwing them into roles of oversight and responsibilities such as discipling can damage the health of the church (Matthew 13:5-6, 20-21). If you are going to err on the side of choosing elders too slowly or too quickly, err on the side of deciding too slowly, especially with new believers.

Well-respected by outsiders (1 Timothy 3:7). Often it is not our Christian brothers and sisters who can give us the best assessment of a potential elder. Those outside our church and outside the faith—our neighbors, coworkers, friends and acquaintances—can offer a more accurate assessment of the character of potential elders.

- Do they love others well outside of times when the church gathers?

- Do they treat their neighbors with respect; do they love and care for them?

- Do they treat their coworkers with care and respect?

- Do they struggle to submit to those in authority?

An elder's character on Sunday must be consistent with their character on the other six days of the week.

2. Family qualifications. Leading well within one's immediate family can be a litmus test for how a potential elder will lead the family of God.

The husband of one wife (1 Timothy 3:2). Longstanding, committed marriages are expressions of healthy relationships, so it is no surprise that Paul wrote about the importance of marriage in elder qualifications. When asked what the most radical thing a Christian could do in the twenty-first century, Eugene Peterson answered, "Be in one, faithful, loving, monogamous relationship your entire life." Modeling faithfulness with a spouse is a great way to model for others what it means to love your most immediate neighbor as yourself.[2]

They must manage their household well (1 Timothy 3:4-5; Titus 1:6). Paul writes that the management of the household should be done "with all dignity keeping his children submissive" (1 Timothy 3:4 ESV).

- How does the family view him?

- Are his children disobedient or significantly lacking wisdom?

- Is she heavy-handed, domineering or authoritative in her parenting style?

- Does he have a desire to discipline his family, and does he deliberately do it?

- What would a spouse and children want to share with the elder about his or her life?

- Is there dignity and respect extended from parent to child and from child to parent?

Paul asks a significant rhetorical question: if a person cannot manage a family household wisely, what makes us think he will manage the family of God wisely? There are several interpretations of what should disqualify an elder from the role (unique circumstances of divorce, children who aren't following the Lord and so on). Paul does not spell out exactly what this means for us, knowing each family situation has its own elements, personalities and situations.

We want to offer an important thought: many parents seem to do all the right things in raising their children in the way of the Lord, yet their children want nothing to do with Christ. Nobody can force someone—including their own child—to follow Christ; everyone must come to that decision on their own terms and of their own volition. Should a wayward child and her actions be held against a potential elder? We believe it is important to focus on the posture, motivations, desires and actions of potential elders in relation to what they can control in their family context.

3. Moral qualifications.

Above reproach (1 Timothy 3:2; Titus 1:6-7). This qualification is not only listed first in both passages, it is also mentioned two times in the Titus passage. Being above reproach does not mean being perfect; it means there is no suspicion of a deeply flawed character. If elders are not trustworthy, we cannot assume they are worth following.

Temperate (1 Timothy 3:2). Sometimes this phrase is translated as *sober-minded*. Some call this "mental sobriety." These people are disciplined and balanced. They think clearly and carefully about issues and refuse to make rash, hasty or unwise decisions that are easily questioned by others. Since many of the decisions made among elders carry significant weight, sober-minded judgment is crucial for wise leadership.

Self-controlled (1 Timothy 3:2; Titus 1:8). Similar to a sober-minded leader, a self-controlled leader is disciplined, realizing that no one is more difficult to lead than one's own self. These leaders exhibit control over their tongues, finances, sexuality, bodies, responsibilities and time. Proverbs 25:28 says, "Like a city whose walls are broken down is a man who lacks self-control." Being sober-minded eliminates the potential for laziness or sloppiness and keeps leaders from lashing out, exploding in anger or making rash decisions that are regretted. An out-of-control leader is a liability.

Respectable (1 Timothy 3:2). Respectable leaders receive respect from others because they live with integrity. They earn credibility over time through their consistent acts of goodness. They are honorable and upright, making appropriate decisions and treating others with respect. Without respect, your leadership as an elder is by title only.

Hospitable (1 Timothy 3:2). Hospitality is not simply inviting people into your home for a wonderful home-cooked meal (though that certainly can be part of it). Hospitality is a generous posture of helping others feel comfortable in new environments. Elders can open their homes regularly to welcome new Christians and hear their stories, to welcome struggling Christians in order to care for and pray for them and to invite faithful Christians to be in relationship with them in order to encourage and thank them for serving in the church. In these spaces of hospitality, elders exhibit shepherd hearts by caring for the flock in highly relational and informal ways.

Gentle (1 Timothy 3:3). It is difficult to be a good shepherd if you are harsh with the sheep. Gentleness, an expression of the Spirit's indwelling in the life of a Christian, is being kind, gracious and compassionate (Galatians 5:22-23). We have all experienced pleasant tenderness and kindness when we have been around gentle leaders. In Philippians 4:5, Paul encourages the church by saying, "Let your gentleness be evident to all." He certainly is not advocating spineless leadership, nor is he asking for cowardly leaders. There are tough situations and decisions that must be made with bold action and tough love, but even those difficult situations can be handled with gentleness. Elders cannot be heavy-handed, mean-spirited, harsh or verbally biting. In doing so, they would not be respectable or self-controlled.

A lover of good (Titus 1:8). This trait is too often overlooked. It is one thing to be good, but it is quite another to be a lover of good. This, too, is one of the evidences of the Spirit (Galatians 5:22-23). Seek out leaders who pursue goodness purposefully and proactively. Being good carries a passive connotation, but being a lover of goodness involves an active pursuit.

Upright (Titus 1:8). This relates closely to remaining above reproach and respectable. *Upright* is also translated as "just" or "righteous." The Scriptures speak of how God's heart longs to bless the lives of righteous people. How does a person lead effectively within a church, in all truth and compassion, when he is unjust and unrighteous?

Holy (Titus 1:8). Similar to being upright, a life marked with devout holiness is fueled by humility and absent of a spirit of pious condescension. Elders who pursue holiness show a church what it means to be set apart for God's work. As Peter writes, "But just as he who called you is holy, so be holy in all you do; for it is written: 'Be holy, because I am holy'" (1 Peter 1:15-16).

Disciplined (Titus 1:8). Being disciplined is closely related to being sober-minded and self-controlled. The role of elder can be demanding. Remaining physically, emotionally, spiritually, financially and vocationally disciplined is important. Do they push themselves even when they don't have to? This is not a matter of being type-A, driven people, but of not being lazy or irresponsible.

Not a drunkard (1 Timothy 3:3; Titus 1:7). Avoiding drunkenness is a moral characteristic evidenced in a specific situational expression of self-control. Certainly Paul does not state that drinking is wrong, but that drinking in excess is. When alcohol controls leaders, they are no longer controlled by God, who dwells inside of them (Ephesians 5:15-18). Refraining from drinking excessively reveals wisdom and self-control.

Not violent (1 Timothy 3:3; Titus 1:7). In addition to addressing how we handle alcohol, Paul tells us that self-control is revealed in how we handle our tempers. It is also closely related to gentleness. Are potential elders easily irritated, or do they have a bad temper? Steer clear. We are called to feed and lead the sheep, not to harass or beat them.

Not quarrelsome (1 Timothy 3:3). In the Beatitudes, Jesus taught that peacemakers are blessed. Keeping peace is quite different than making peace. Seek out leaders who seek out peace. If a potential elder is quarrelsome, that can indicate a spirit of division and a lack of patience and maturity. Quarrelsomeness is a significant character flaw that usually surfaces in damaging ways, especially during times of conflict. If unity is what you are striving for on your elder team and in your church, Paul's warning is crucial (see 2 Timothy 2:24-25). Divisive spirits wreak havoc in a church—especially on an elder team. An elder must be able to address and deal with conflict, not add to it.

Not a lover of money (1 Timothy 3:3). Possessing money and loving money are two different things (see 1 Timothy 6:6-10). The difference is in the desire and the motivation behind money and the pursuit of it. In his first letter to Timothy, Paul writes of the importance of contentment. The unhealthy pursuit of money, Paul says, leads into many foolish and harmful desires that plunge people into ruin and destruction. His words are gripping: "Some people, eager for money, have wandered from the faith and pierced themselves with many griefs" (1 Timothy 6:10). What a striking image being "pierced . . . with many griefs" is! A love of money can appear in subtle and dramatic ways, but whatever its expression, it can derail a church's desire to pursue God's mission.

Not overbearing (Titus 1:7). Arrogant elders are the most destructive kind. All it takes is one strong-willed and self-centered elder who strong-arms their way through decisions or situations to damage—if not destroy—the unity and trust of an elder team. Humility is one of the keystone characteristics among elders, since so many of the negative characteristics to avoid hinge on this directive. If humility is evident in an elder's life, most of the negative characteristics will assuredly be absent. Are potential elders defensive, haughty, seeking the attention of others or bragging—even if in veiled ways? A qualified elder humble enough to lead does not demand respect from people. The moment an elder—or any leader—demands respect from those he is leading is the moment respect diminishes dramatically.

Not quick-tempered (Titus 1:7). Often those who are easily angered feel as though they have to defend themselves. This can often reveal a heart full of pride. James wrote that we are to be "quick to listen, slow to speak and slow to become angry" (James 1:19). Loose cannons should be avoided. Attacks, accusations and tense moments come with their territory. Elders dealing with difficult and sensitive situations should diffuse drama, not add to it.

Elders as Carriers of Vision

After reading the qualifications of an elder, an important question must be considered: who wouldn't want to follow and submit to this type of leader? These leaders have attractive lives, thus making Christ who resides in them attractive to others.

Three quarters of the biblical qualifications given in 1 Timothy and Titus focus on character, not ability.[3] Why does Paul spell out these qualifications in such great detail? Because *elders are carriers of vision within a local church.* Howard Hendricks said the number-one problem of spiritual leaders in America is a lack of character. Nothing can derail the mission of a church more significantly than unqualified—or disqualified—leaders overseeing a church.

Undoubtedly, elders faithfully engaged in people's lives find it to be quite messy. Elders learn things about people they don't always want to know: struggling marriages, financial ruin, sinful patterns, sexual sins, poor decision making, addictions, abuse, broken relationships and immaturity. It takes a great amount of patience, integrity, maturity, faith and godly character to handle these situations wisely while also using discretion regarding what to do with such information.

Finally, it is important to remember the source of an elder's calling and authority. The authority to become an elder is not from other elders or the church as a whole. It comes from the Holy Spirit (Acts 20:28). People should not submit to the elders in their church just because they hold the title of elder. Elders have the responsibility to shepherd the congregation well, an authority given by God himself.[4] Remember: *elders help lead the church, but Christ remains the head.*

5

Cultivating an Ethos
Rooted in God's Mission

*Apostolic leaders understand that what God is creating is a
community with a cause. Both the needs of the community
and the sacrifice necessary to accomplish the cause are clearly
before them. It is through such leadership that movement is
initiated. Fueled by faith, these leaders move forward to
accomplish the purpose of God.*

ERWIN MCMANUS, *AN UNSTOPPABLE FORCE*

As the Father has sent me, I am sending you.

JESUS, IN JOHN 20:21

THE FOUR STATUES

About half a mile north of the iconic Philadelphia Museum of Art
on Kelly Drive, just past Boathouse Row, is the Ellen Phillips
Samuel Memorial Terrace. On the terrace stand four granite
statues about twelve feet in height, erected in the 1950s. Each was

created by a different artist and looks out over the Schuylkill River, displaying four striking postures.[1]

- The first statue, a steel worker with a clenched jaw, welding mask, protective gloves and boots, carries a description on its base: "Laborer: He Wrought Miracles."

- The second, a serious-looking man holding a scientific tool for measurement in one hand and leaning on a larger tool with his left, reads, "Scientist: He Weighed the Stars."

- The third figure, which has feminine facial features, wears a long, flowing robe. She holds a scroll across her heart, with the description "Poet: He Shaped Our Dreams."

- And, the last statue, a minister in preaching robes with knees bent leans forward with the description "Preacher: He Guided Our Ways."

But the posture of the last statue is jarringly different from what would be expected. His hands are cupped, not around his mouth, but around his left ear, with his head tilted to the side so as to listen carefully. His eyes are open wide and his mouth is slightly open; his forearms draw the eye's attention up to his ear. It is a powerful image: a preacher whose primary posture is that of listening. On occasion, I (J.R.) travel to the plaza and sit with my journal at the base of the listening preacher. I do this to consider what this posture has to teach me as a church leader.[2]

Though these four statues were created with the intent of expressing the spirit of the city of Philadelphia, I have found few symbols that communicate the essence of Christian ministry more clearly. The roles and postures of a mission-shaped elder are laborer, scientist, poet and preacher—each expression distinct, yet interrelated.

- We are laborers, working diligently to shepherd God's people faithfully.

- We are scientists, studying and exhibiting the deep truths of the good news of Jesus.

- We are poets, cultivating environments of inspiration and shaping the kingdom imaginations of our people.

- And we are preachers, taking a humble posture of learning and listening, absent of condescension, so as to proclaim the message of the gospel in our context.

What do we listen to—and what do we *not* listen to? We listen, first and foremost, to the Spirit, who guides his church. We also listen to the culture—not to imitate its ways, but to lead shrewdly and compassionately, wisely translating God's Word into that culture. Like the men of Issachar who understood what Israel was to do, we seek to be people who understand the times in order to know what we should do in our contexts (1 Chronicles 12:32). This posture is not a direct denial of or an embrace of culture, but a deep awareness of our need to engage with it.

In our minds is the question "How does the gospel speak into *this* situation?" Graham Buxton writes that the challenge of leadership is to engage the world in such a way as to retain both cultural relevance and gospel faithfulness, without falling into either cultural naiveté or dogmatic fundamentalism.[3]

When we listen to each other as elders, we model unity and deepen trust. When we listen to the people within our local churches, we exhibit humility, build trust and shepherd compassionately. We fulfill our roles as spiritual leaders by paying attention to God and learning to respond appropriately. We cannot shepherd, oversee, teach, equip and model a mission-directed ethos rooted in Jesus without listening to the Spirit, to God's Word, to each other, to our people and to those outside of a life with Christ.

THE DRIVING FORCE OF ETHOS

The fundamental nature of culture—its powerful undercurrents of values, beliefs and practices—cannot be ignored. The composition of any family, organization, business or church is significant to its specific mission. One of the most significant roles of leaders is *to cultivate a culture that aligns with the church's mission.* Paul worked hard to communicate the importance of identifying the right leaders to lead local church expressions, because he knew the power that leaders have in cultivating and shaping culture. Mission-shaped leaders cultivate mission-directed culture.

DNA is cellular and microscopic. Doctors and biologists tell us that if we are healthy on the cellular level our entire body will be healthy. The same is true for the culture of your church. When elders focus on the cellular health in the DNA of a church, it has significant implications on the overall health of the church. To grow big, you have to grow small.

Ethos and culture are wrapped up in what a particular group holds most dear. The ethos may not always be easily discernible, but it is always present. The ethos of a subgroup is an understood (though not always overtly expressed) value system, a relational contract of interaction. Certain questions reveal ethos:

- What do we celebrate in our culture? What do we mourn?

- What is taboo? What are sacred cows?

- What language do we use to describe how we see the world? What distinct elements of our vernacular reveal what we value?

- What stories are legends—told over and over again—and why do we tell these particular stories?

Churches often become what their leaders are. This can be both beneficial and dangerous. The most effective way to see your church embrace a culture centered on Jesus and aligned with his mission is to have your elders live it out. Churches with a mission-driven ethos seek out the best leaders in a church in order to create a culture that encourages movement toward the heart of God. Just as children carry the DNA of their parents and pick up on their mannerisms, mission-shaped elders carry the DNA of our mission-originating Father and mimic his mannerisms, revealing his heart in us and in the people in our churches. We must create a culture that discourages the cultural expectation that leaders operate as busy salespeople on God's behalf.

The what, who, why and how a church values say something significant about its ethos. The way a church greets one another says something about community. The way a church prays together says something about faith and humility. The way a church responds to crisis and sin says something about grace. The way a church mourns says something about compassion. And the way a church worships says something about what we believe about God. Structure is important, but it is rooted in an ethos. Structure is largely influenced by your current ethos—or what you desire the ethos of your church to be. Too many churches over-emphasize structure and thus underemphasize ethos. Above all, create a culture that cares the most about the things Jesus cares the most about, regardless of what your structure is.

THE LANGUAGE WE USE

What we do informs and impacts culture, but so does how we communicate. Language creates culture. The accepted language of specific people groups and subcultures matters—and it matters to your church. For example, what do you call your elders? When we use the term "elder board," it may lead people to think of a board meeting in a corporate setting. It may also encourage a culture of corporate leadership carried out only by the experts and professionals. It would stress the role of overseer, but could potentially minimize that of shepherd or teacher.

New Testament churches used the language of family and body. It may be wise to consider calling your elders "the elder team" or simply "the elders." Since one of the primary roles of an elder is to equip, we have heard of churches that refer to their elders as "equippers."

Whatever you end up calling your elders, consider these questions:

- If a significant metaphor used for a church in the New Testament for church is family, how might our language capture this idea of family in a clear and compelling fashion, especially as we think about those in leadership of the family?

- Since relationships are so crucial in the gospel story and in the context of a church, how might we use language that reflects a high value for relationships?

- How might our language regarding leadership be reflected in our actions—and vice versa?

We don't want to split hairs about every possible word you could use, but we advocate for a purposeful use of language. Simply changing the language or wording won't change the culture entirely, but using purposeful and descriptive language helps to cast a clear vision and direction, which assists in the development of an ethos that aligns with God's mission.

MISSION-SATURATED ETHOS

An ethos saturated in the mission of God focuses less on developing high-quality programs and more on encouraging faith-filled participation with the Spirit—both with those who know Christ and those who do not yet know him.

An ethos that prioritizes God's mission is not rooted in doing things *for* God. Instead, the stress is on ministry *with, through* and *in* him. When we do things *for* God, it can become burdensome and legalistic and can lack life and freedom. Yet when we attempt to lead, allowing him to work *with, through* and *in* us, it is a deep privilege and joy.

The word *culture* comes from the Latin word *cultura,* which means "to cultivate." We have to think less like engineers and organizational architects and more like ecologists and gardeners. Spiritual leaders are kingdom horticulturalists. Disciples are not mass-produced, built on an assembly line in a factory or warehouse. They are attended to and cultivated in the messiness and mundaneness of life. Ecology requires a different approach than engineering.

This ethos refuses to be comfortable with being comfortable—a difficult task in a culture saturated with comfort and convenience. But stability, comfort and convenience were never terms Paul had in mind when writing his letters to churches. Elders cannot cater to the preferences of the people who show up at church and declare, "We are looking for a church that meets our needs." We must fight the temptation to breed a culture of consumerism in our churches. A consumer orientation and a mission orientation are incompatible, and the best way to slay the beast of consumerism is to starve it.

Alan Hirsch writes that every follower of Christ involved in a local church should ask, "Is this 'a community for me' or is this 'me for the community and the community for the sake of the world'?"[4] One of the most important roles an elder can play in the life of the church is to continually remind her people that church is not a self-seeking venture. Healthy leaders raise the spiritual temperature of the ethos of a local church, reminding people it's not about their preferences, but about Christ's purposes.

It's not about asking, "How can we make our church grow?" but instead about asking, "How do we care about the things

Jesus cared about most?" It's prioritizing growing hearts and people's character over growing budgets and attendance. God longs to see people who grow to love him and who seek to be allies and advocates for others in the name of Jesus.

Many Christians in North America are educated well beyond their level of obedience. The gap between knowledge and application is significant. If the church truly is the tangible, local, redemptive agent of God, seek to cultivate a purposeful community of obedience as a respite *for* the world, not a respite *from* it. Make the sacrifice: put a greater emphasis on transformation than on information.

THE IMPORTANCE OF ADAPTABILITY

One of the most important elements of a mission-informed ethos is adaptability. If we are seeking the Spirit, who is described as an unpredictable wind, we must be ready to follow wherever that wind may be blowing. This can be unnerving for a team of elders who are concerned about issues such as the budget, programs, attendance and the maintenance of facilities. But it would be unwise to create a new wineskin and tell God what kind of wine to fill it with. We want to see what kind of wine God provides and have a wineskin—our structure—that is pliable and flexible enough to wrap around his new work. The only way our structure can do this is if our ethos encourages such adaptability. The structure must always submit to the Spirit. In short, it's a commitment to build floating docks.

A few years ago, my wife bought a gallon of milk at Costco, which had recently redesigned the shape for its milk containers. The spout was larger and the container taller and skinnier, giving it a more cylindrical shape. Costco told consumers the new shape allowed for easier, more efficient stocking and delivery, and was more cost-effective. There was only one problem: when we poured the milk from the container, it hugged the side of the container, spilled all over the kitchen counter and made a mess. We estimated more milk spilled on the kitchen counter than ended up in our glasses and cereal bowls. It was our first—and last—time buying milk at Costco. And thousands of people have expressed the same frustration online.

While Costco may have developed a new, innovative design, created a more efficient shipping and delivery process, and saved a few pennies with each purchase, they forgot the whole point: the milk needs to pour from the container into a glass or bowl. They forgot the most important thing: it's about the milk, not the container. The container merely holds the milk and assists in the pouring.

If we're not careful, we can come to believe that the container (the church's structure) is more important than the milk (the Spirit's work). We renovate our buildings, develop more efficient systems and create attractive programs, but we forget the purpose of the church: allowing the Spirit to pour himself into us and through us as we love and serve a broken world. What we need is not new and innovative designs and more efficient processes, but a clear commitment to allowing God's Spirit to pour freely in and through our churches. Our structures must adapt in order to allow the Spirit to be accessible to the people in our context.

To many, structuring for mission sounds good, but when it comes down to it, a significant culture change requires a great amount of courage, risk and sacrifice on the part of church leadership. We like our milk containers. Respecting our histories is one thing; attempting to turn back the clock and return to the glory days out of self-preservation is quite another.

Certainly, we stand on the shoulders of women and men who have gone before us. Much can and should be gleaned from their faithful way of life (see Hebrews 11). But we cannot dwell on or glorify the past. God desires to do more and to break into new areas, places and people groups with new and creative expressions. Mission-oriented elders create a floating dock ethos that is less interested in preserving the past and more interested in making an investment that impacts the future for God's glory.

The last thing a mission-rooted church needs is domesticated elders. We serve a God of incredible power, creativity and compassion, and our job is to reflect his heart clearly to a world desperately in need of an encounter with such a God. The Holy Spirit is already actively at work in the world in which we live; our responsibility is to join him in it, no matter what it might cost.

CULTIVATING AN ETHOS OF HEALTH

An ethos fueled by mission places more value on health than on growth. A byproduct of health is growth—not the other way around. Therefore, proactively promoting emotional, mental, physical, relational and spiritual health—especially among elders—is crucial to the overall health of the church. If an elder team is to be a micro-community of a healthy church and a model for the entire community, its elders must strive for health.

CARING FOR EACH OTHER

With issues of sin, conflict, immaturity and dissension—sometimes coming at breakneck speed and frequency—elders can feel the brunt of the sin and brokenness within a church. Many decisions are incredibly delicate and, at times, extremely awkward. These weighty issues can affect the elders' spouses and children too. If elders are constantly giving without being cared for, they can dry up. But if elders are built into, cared for and equipped, they are able to give of themselves to the church—even when it feels intense.

How might the elders of your church be cared for so they can care for others?

- What if we cared more about balanced relationships in our church—and among our elders—than about balance sheets?

- How might we be equipped so we can best equip the saints?

- How might we receive training so we can train our people to remain on mission?

We ought to offer practical opportunities to care for, equip and train each other as elders, so that we can be best equipped for our roles. Cultivating a healthy ethos means building in time, space and expectation to care for each other, even though the agenda is full. This may mean a longer, less efficient elder meeting, but it may encourage a caring environment where burdens are shared, just as you'd like to see your church embody.

PRACTICAL WAYS TO CARE FOR ONE ANOTHER

Invest deeply in each other's lives. Elders can share joys and anxieties, laughter and tears. They can vent to one another and share stories of great joy. Certainly, it is far more efficient to start a meeting immediately by addressing issues on the agenda, but it is far more effective to be involved in each other's lives— to know how our families and jobs and friends are doing. This also lessens the perception that we have to be efficient so we can be most effective.

Pray with and for one another. We care for each other by praying for one another—our hurts, our burdens, our work, our children, our health—and for unity as an elder team. With this comes confession too. Few things help us carry our burdens with one another more than when we confess our sins to one another. We do all we can to avoid the seemingly obligatory and predictably unmemorable times of opening prayer and closing prayer.

Soak in the waters of the Scriptures together. We also build into the beginning of the agenda time in the Scriptures. In a rotation, each elder takes the responsibility every few elder meetings to lead a time of reflection in Scripture. This allows us to shepherd one another.

Check in with one another outside meetings. Sending text messages, making phone calls and sending emails where the intent is simply to check in can be a normal part of the culture of your elders. On occasion, I drop by briefly to see one of our elders who owns a small business a few miles from my house. At other times I have lunch with an elder to simply ask how they are doing—not even mentioning the church.

Spend time together. Build in time outside normally scheduled meetings to connect. Going out to dinner, enjoying dessert, going for a hike, spending a day at the beach or hanging out on the back porch can cultivate a spirit of relationships that run much deeper than business-only interactions.

Make sacrifices for each other. Caring includes making sacrifices, even at the expense of your elder team. Several years ago, Jon, one of our (J.R.'s) elders, who specifically oversaw worship in our weekend gatherings, dealt with a severe health issue in his family. His wife, Karrie, had a brain aneurism and spent a few months in an ICU. By God's grace, she survived but required an extreme amount of care, attention and help. In addition to his wife, their three young children were in need of constant care. We rallied our church to make meals, babysit and run errands for Karrie, since she was not permitted to drive. Many made financial contributions to provide for a babysitter so Jon could maintain his work schedule at a steel mill.

We spoke with Jon and asked if it would be best if he were released from his responsibilities as elder so he could focus on caring for his family. He told us he loved being a part of the elder team, but he felt that being released from that responsibility—at least for the time being—would be best for his family. Though we continue to miss him in his official role as elder, we knew it was best for him to step away indefinitely to care for his family. The offer for Jon to step back into an official role of elder is still open, and we ask the question in each new ministry season.

Protect and hold one another accountable. Holding one another accountable is an important way to care for one another. It also provides built-in protection against accusation. For example, all of our elders have installed the Internet accountability software Covenant Eyes on their computers.[5] Do any of our elders have an Internet issue or a pornography addiction? No, but this is a way we can model to our community what it means to be above reproach in this critical area. This accountability is not based in fear, but is to protect our unity and credibility and to protect against false accusations that might be leveled against an elder.

Training and Equipping

Health and maturity also include growing in knowledge and wisdom as elders. Training and equipping can occur in a variety of ways—both formally and informally. Simply asking your elders where they feel ill equipped or where they believe they need more training in their roles is important. If you are a staff pastor or church planter, it is important for you to have a pulse on the life of your elders, especially those who are nonstaff elders. Seek out ways to ask them how they hope to be trained, where they feel they are lacking and where they feel the entire elder team is lacking.

Formal training may include attending conferences together, inviting wise outside voices in to speak to your situation or hiring an experienced mission-oriented consultant who can administer an analysis or assessment of your church's health. Some elder teams go on an annual or semiannual overnight retreat together. Getting out of the area, spending unrushed time together, praying together, sharing meals and discussing significant topics (especially those that need a longer period than a normal elder meeting would allow) provides a clearer perspective, creates deeper relational bonds, offers significant times of prayer, allows elders to make memories and facilitates significant decisions that impact the church. Informal training may involve reading articles or links, swapping books or watching training material together.

6

Selecting Elders

People will follow you for a while because they picked you.
But they'll follow you over the long term because
they have learned to trust you.

GORDON MacDONALD

Paul and Barnabas appointed elders for them in each
church and, with prayer and fasting, committed them
to the Lord, in whom they had put their trust.

ACTS 14:23

⫸⫷

Twice in ministry I (Bob) have seen recalcitrant elders hamstring pastors. These elders represented the old guard within their church—those who believed things were fine as they were and resisted any forward movement in terms of mission and vision. In both cases, the pastor cited the headache of dealing with someone stubbornly opposed to him as a prime reason he left the church.

At other times, I've seen pastors saddled with elders who, while genuinely godly and loving people, were by no means prepared to lead. Their election to the board seemed to be based solely on their willingness to serve, as opposed to bringing something valuable to the team. As a result, their presence was neutral at best, but often became a hindrance, as the real work of shepherding and leadership had to be divided among the remaining elders. As we discussed earlier, they were willing but unable.

Few actions will have a more significant impact on the life of your church than the selection of your elder team. These are the ones who lead, pray for, work for and teach your community. Conversely, if you are going to see a shadow side to leadership express itself, it's often on the elder team, and it often manifests with an elder who seems set on opposing the pastor, opposing forward movement—opposing everything, really. For reasons both practical and biblical, we advise against eldership being determined by elections. Instead, we recommend that the elders on your team be determined by a careful, prayerful process that includes the whole community, but is primarily driven by the current elders.

APPOINTMENT VS. ELECTION

"We need someone to represent our side." "No one else is running, so . . ." "He's just such a nice man." These rationales are often heard when choosing elders. Unfortunately, none of them is a reason someone should be an elder.

On the surface, the election of elders makes sense in our democratic society. It seems to provide checks and balances, a way for the voice of the congregation to be heard and a balanced means of choosing elders. And in a perfect church, all those would be true. Elders would be chosen without regard for factions, but rather as a means to shore up the weaknesses and enhance the strengths of the current team.

However, in practice, the opposite is often true. Rather than shoring up the weaknesses of a team, elections can exacerbate divisions as new personalities and agendas are thrust onto the team. All this to say, elections rarely (and only with significant forethought) provide the humble, robust servant team a church needs.

Who Appoints the First Elders of a New Community?

There are three options in creating an elder-led community.

The first involves a sending church. As it appoints a planter to go and seed a new community, it also appoints elders to join in the task. While this would be ideal, it takes an extraordinary church community to send not only a church planter but also elder-level leaders. Our hope would be that more and more churches would not only see the need for new communities and move to meet it, but also invest in the leadership of those new communities in this way.

The second option is what most often happens. A solo church planter decides to plant a community from scratch and needs to find leaders to join and help with the work of ministry. While this is more daunting, don't miss the inherent spiritual formation this provides for the church community. In Luke 10:2, Jesus encourages us to pray for workers to help in the fields, but few of us take this to heart until we're forced to by something like the glaring need for leaders for a new community.

This second scenario means that together with your core team, you choose from among yourselves those you see as gifted, qualified and eager to help shepherd your new community. Using the processes outlined above and below, move through this together, appointing the first elders of your new community.

Third, what of a core team that has not quite gelled and is not quite in a place to work through an elder process together?

Often the responsibility of appointing the elders of a new community falls squarely on the shoulders of the founding church planter/pastor. If you are the church planter or founding pastor of the church, it's your responsibility to appoint others. Do this carefully, as it will be one of the prime factors in establishing the DNA of your new church community.

What should be done when, in looking out at your new congregation, you see no qualified elder candidates—or no one that is likely to be ready any time soon? In this case, new congregations should consider developing what is called a provisional elder team. It should be comprised of wise pastors outside of your church who know you and believe in the mission of your new church start. They offer big-picture oversight, experience, prayer, encouragement and direction for the pastor for a short time. Some of the issues may include feedback, offering their own wisdom and experience regarding ministry and leadership practices, and soul care. Usually a pastor serves on a provisional elder team for a few months or up to a couple of years until new elders are identified, trained and commissioned. They do not normally get involved in the lives of the people in that congregation (due to the fact that these pastors are busy serving in their own congregations).

Provisional elder teams may meet once a month or quarterly. Though less hands-on, they meet to help cultivate the big-picture mission and vision of the new church. While provisional elders can be anywhere, it makes the most sense to have them in the region or in the context where your new church will be planted. In addition to occasional meetings, it may be wise to reach out to individual provisional elders via phone, email or in person to ask specific questions or for those provisional elders to ask questions about the overall health of the pastor, the pastor's family and the congregation. If their time and schedule allows, have them attend a service or event to get the feel of the community and possibly to speak, teach or preach so the people in the new church can become familiar with the provisional elders.

As new elders within the congregation are identified, trained and commissioned, provisional elders may end their official involvement. It would be wise to consider a weaning on/weaning off process, having some provisional elders and new elders overlap to provide stability, consistency and clear communication with the new congregation.

In addition to provisional elders, we highly recommend securing a church-planting coach who is capable of offering wisdom, insight, resources and contacts that will help you as you establish elders and develop a mission culture.

How Soon?

One of the top mistakes a new church can make is to formalize leadership too soon. Some of the best advice we can give is to be very patient when bringing on elders at the start. See it as a marathon, not a sprint. The cement is wet; make sure you let it set so it becomes a firm foundation that will last for years to come. Fight the temptation to be hasty in making decisions on elders. Be wise, patient, cautious and prayerful about it. It will have an incredible impact on your church culture.

However, we have seen churches well into their third year of being a community together still without elders, and we don't think this is in any way healthy. Appointing elders too quickly can lead to immaturity in a team and waiting too long can be detrimental to the health of the community.

Bill Easum and Bill Griffith, in their helpful book *Ten Mistakes New Church Starts Make and How to Avoid Them*, share that leaders must prove themselves within the church. It's wise to say that we ought to give leadership to people who have proven themselves in our church, not in someone else's church.

That way, the congregation gets to see firsthand a leader's traits and character. Discovering leaders happens over time.

Our recommendation is to find the sweet spot between "carefully" and "expeditiously" in a new church community. Don't delay the elder process for years, but don't rush the process once it's started. Ideally, you'll launch your church community with one or two co-elders in your core team or be in process with it as you begin. Barring that, do your best to have at least a couple of elders in place no longer than a year or so after launching a new community.

If your structure is one where you are required to have a "management team" of outside people who act as your board (this is often done for a three-year period), do your best to raise up an elder team alongside them.[1] Your management team may resist calling this group "elders," but local, from-the-community leadership is so vital, we'd advise doing whatever you can, within the constraints placed on you, to create an indigenous leadership team that functions as the on-the-ground leadership of your community until you are released by your management team to form an elder board.

A Process for Selecting Elders

Again, selecting elders, whether through election or appointment, should be a process—and by definition, not a short one. There are a lot of things you can and should do quickly in the life of your church. Choosing what website hosting you will use and what your logo will be, developing financial systems and protocols—all of these things can be decided rather quickly, tried and changed later if found not to work well. With elders, however, it's a different story entirely. A quick decision or one left to chance can hamstring not only an elder team but a whole community. Don't take shortcuts on the process.

Step 1: Cultivation. Look around your community. Do you see people you think would make good elders one day? Have you expressed that to them? Many never consider leading a community as an elder because no one has "called it out" of them. No one has said, "I see God's hand on you, your growing maturity and wisdom, and your presence in our community. I'd like to see you someday become an elder, and here are the steps that I think would make that possible."

There are people on my (Bob's) elder team now because, four years before they started serving in that role, I had a conversation with them where I painted an arc of growth and maturity for them that culminated in serving as an elder. Others we had to ask multiple times; when we decided we would like to see them on the team, they just weren't ready for various reasons. Keeping folks who say "not now" or "not yet" on the cultivation list is a way of participating in what God is doing in their lives. Continue to pray with them, give them opportunities for growth and service or even just give them space not to serve for a season, and continue to offer invitations to consider eldership.

Then there are others who take to heart the biblical statement that those who aspire to being an elder desire a noble thing, and they make it clear to you or someone on your team that they would like to serve in this way. This is your chance to speak into their spiritual formation, to ask and consider why they want to serve in that way, what's kept them from being considered up to that point and how they might need to grow to get there. Then you can communicate clearly and lovingly the growth process you'd like to see for them.

Step 2: Consideration. At least once a year, we look around and say, "Who is doing the work of an elder already? Who is getting there? Who would we like to see on this track?" We make a mental list of those we see moving toward eldership and those who are now actively being elder-ish in our community. We discuss not only who seem to be the wise, respected people in our community but also who seem to be at a place in life where eldership would make sense, as well as who seem to be a good fit with our current team: Who would round us out? Who seems to get where we're going? Who do we feel drawn to invite?

As a team, we also carefully consider those who are suggested by the community. Though we have no set "nomination" process, we often receive feedback that a particular person would make a great elder. We take that statement from the community seriously, though never as a mandate. Often members of the community can see a person serving and being a wise presence in ways we as an elder team can't. They see who is leading in their home community, who is loving and serving others. This feedback is often extremely valuable in helping us see those who are already "eldering" under the radar.

Also, it's helpful to determine who's more of a deacon than an elder. Those who are serving their hearts out in the community are often mentioned as potential elders. Take into account not merely who is serving well in task-oriented, deacon-level types of ministry (leading the setup team, initiating a justice-oriented ministry, taking meals to those who need them), but also who is spiritually mature enough not just to serve but to guide, not just to put into practice what we're teaching but to teach others as well. That's an elder. Be sure you know the difference.

Step 3: Invitation. When we have decided that we are ready to invite people into the elder process, we usually have someone contact them to determine their willingness. Often we need to give them time to think, pray and talk with a spouse or spiritual director. And we make sure we are clear: we are inviting them into a process of discernment with us. This may or may not lead to serving on the elder team, and there's no commitment involved in entering the process. We just want to hear together what God may be saying about them serving in this way.

Step 4: Qualification. The invitation, if accepted, moves to a season of discernment together. The person being invited is asked to do a self-evaluation against the qualifications of an elder found in 1 Timothy and Titus. The current elder team is also asked to consider this person vis-à-vis these qualifications, as described in an earlier chapter.

Step 5: Interviews. After a time (usually a month or so) of thinking and praying through the qualifications of an elder, if the person being considered feels confident about the process, we schedule a time to meet with the whole elder team—usually an hour out of a regular elders meeting. This could also be a special meeting dedicated to interviews, particularly if you have more than one person in the process.

During this interview time, we want to hear what was brought up internally as the candidates considered the qualifications. Where do they feel strong, and where do they see a need for growth? Was there anything uncovered they feel might have the potential to disqualify them? We also give our feedback in terms of how we see them, how they are gifted and how they match up in terms of the qualifications. Even if the process doesn't end with someone becoming an elder, this time is usually a great encouragement for everyone involved, as we are able to affirm someone's giftedness and contributions to the community.

Some other things we want to hear include their spiritual journey: how did they come to follow Jesus and what is their story of growth and maturity, along with their struggles? We especially want to hear how they understand the gospel, how they understand and explain the good news to themselves and to others. We want to hear how they evaluate the community: what they love about it; what they would change. How do they see their own giftedness and contributions to the elder team? We ask doctrinal questions, life questions, personal questions— generally speaking, not from a script but as the conversation unfolds and is guided, we hope, by the Holy Spirit. We want to know how their spouse views the potential of them serving in this way, how they will make time and what concerns they have about taking on the role.

These interviews are generally a lot of fun. The person being interviewed often confesses to entering the interview with some trepidation and nervousness, but the laughter and love in the room is always disarming. We pray together, asking for guidance and discernment, and end by asking for permission to interview the person's spouse (if he or she has one) and one or two other significant friends within the church. We want to get a well-rounded view, not just of what they think of themselves and of serving with us, but what others think as well.

Interviewing spouses and friends may seem like a bit much, but trust us: this is vital. We have had significant conversations with spouses that have led us to say something like, "We love who you are and what you would bring to this team, but we sense your spouse already believes you are overworked and overcommitted. We can't in good conscience add to that right now."

Step 6: Presentation. After all the interviews have been completed, if everyone involved feels we have uncovered no red flags and we still want to proceed, we present the potential elder to the community. If you have an elections process, this may look different, but for us, it involves one of the current elders standing up before the community, usually at a Sunday-morning gathering, and saying something like, "We as elders feel that so-and-so is an elder of our community and we'd like to bring her on the team. We've worked through the interview process and feel strongly that she is qualified and gifted to serve in this role. But we'd also like to hear from you. If you feel that this is a good move, tell us. If you feel that for some reason this might be a mistake, we want to hear why. If at the end of two or three weeks, we haven't heard anything that gives us pause, we'll go ahead and bring her on the team."

Often this announcement is greeted with cheers. That's when we know we are doing our job of discerning eldership well.

Step 7: Commissioning/Ordination. We feel it's important to cap off the process with a public laying on of hands. Not only is this biblical, on a practical level it serves the community by conferring a sense of solemnity on the role of elder. It says, this person is agreeing to serve you, teach you, help guide our community; he needs our prayers and our support in this. We generally fold this commissioning into one of our Sunday gatherings as part of our worship.

TERM LIMITS

Should elders serve for set terms or indefinitely? There's wisdom in both approaches. Set terms help people avoid burnout and ensure that we are constantly developing new elders. Yet the gelling of a team is perpetually interrupted when members rotate on and off.

On the other side is the view that once a person is qualified as an elder, he is free to serve in that capacity as long as he remains qualified and willing. For our (Bob's) community, we have no set terms. Rather, elders serve as long as they are willing, often taking a year or two off when family or work necessitates, but always with the idea that they may come back by invitation at a later time. Some churches adopt a required break for elders who have served a certain number of years. But as with the number of elders on your team, we believe the length an elder serves should be directed by the Spirit, not by set policies.

Structure is necessary and helpful, but avoiding overstructure is imperative to a generative, relationally rooted, Spirit-directed faith community focused on mission. What we suggest is another option: pursuing God's heart for the length of each elder's service. While serving indefinitely can have its own set of issues, what is assumed is trust and unity with the Lord—and with each other. If elders are unified and are together seeking God's heart for the church they are entrusted to lead, then serving Christ and pursuing what is best for the health, focus and overall mission of that church is the primary concern. Since elders met the qualifications of spiritual maturity when they were selected and have proven godly character, we assume their maturity will be evident in their ability to discern God's purposes in their leadership as elders. There is no pressure or expectation; there is simply an invitation to listen to the Spirit together.

How to Tell an Elder from a Problem Leader

We wish it didn't need to be said, but it probably does: not everyone who wants to be an elder should be one. As already cited, Scripture says whoever desires to be an elder desires a noble thing. But this doesn't mean it's always desired for noble reasons.

About three years into the life of our church community, our elders were considering why so many churches that had started around the same time were having problems with tough personalities on their elder boards: people who seemed to have an agenda, people who fought the pastor on the vision and mission of the church or people who seemed to enjoy leading a little too much.

We seemed to have avoided this altogether, and after discussing it for a while, we concluded that this was primarily because when people came our church with ministry experience or a theology degree, we didn't rush to put them into authority. Our general practice was to ask them to help set up, move the chairs around, whatever. Those who truly wanted to serve the community rarely had a problem with this; it wasn't *below* them. But some were offended. They felt their degrees and experience entitled them to a position in our community. Those people moved on fairly quickly—most likely to a small church or church plant that would give them what they were looking for.

Our encouragement to you is this: don't be swayed by degrees or past positions. See how people live and serve within your community before you give them a title, especially the title of elder. Let them prove themselves in your community of faith by being faithful with task-oriented jobs before moving them into ministry positions. Make sure they are servants before they become leaders.

We've rarely regretted moving too slowly with someone, but we *have* regretted moving too fast. The position of elder is not something anyone is entitled to. It's something that's discerned in the life of a faithful servant of Jesus who loves a community with his actions and his presence.

IF YOUR CHURCH IS STRUCTURED CONGREGATIONALLY

If your church is constitutionally structured as one that chooses elders by election, there is still great hope that you can have an elder team that moves your community forward in mission and growth toward Christlikeness. But getting there will require great intentionality and sacrifice on the part of the leadership.

First, the community must be educated as to what elders are and do, biblically. They must be encouraged (exhorted even, to use the biblical term) to set aside political agendas and, trusting God, choose godly people over influential, longstanding or "successful" people. They need to be reminded that the wealthiest, the most business-savvy, the most outspoken people in the community may not necessarily be the best suited for the elder team. Wisdom, Christlikeness, humility, concern for mission and unity in the congregation—these are the values to focus on when choosing elders.

We're convinced that if these values are repeatedly stressed and if the congregation prayerfully approaches the election of elders, a great elder team can come together through elections.

Second, putting a few names on a ballot at the yearly business meeting as the third agenda item of ten may not be the best way to select elders. The election of elders calls for a communal process that is set apart in the life of the community and is approached as a holy duty rather than as a necessary evil. The community should be encouraged to feel the weight of responsibility in choosing elders. They ought to review the qualifications found in 1 Timothy and Titus each and every time they approach the choosing of elders and spend time in prayer and discernment. Only after significant consideration of candidates, fearfully and with dependence on God for the furthering of the mission of their community, should they mark a ballot.

Third, it may be that even in a congregational government situation, an elder board can provide great guidance in the selection of elders by interviewing and preapproving candidates. We're struck by how often the election process seems to overlook this vital step. Allow candidates to be nominated, or to nominate themselves, but don't skip the part of the process where those candidates are evaluated (by both themselves and the elder team as a whole) on the qualifications of an elder (see the previous chapter on biblical qualifications for more specifics).

In addition to the godly character laid out in the biblical qualifications, in the interview look for a fit with the team and a commitment to the vision and mission of the church. Use the time to determine what you are hearing from God, as a team, about the potential candidates. Follow the process outlined above, and when you feel you have some great candidates who would be wonderful additions to your team, submit them to the congregation for election.[2]

Will you have some folks who fight this enhanced election process? Probably. But the alternative is risky: an elder team that may or may not have qualified individuals or unity. These things are worth fighting for.

Eldership as
Spiritual Formation

When God works in us nothing is useless,
and nothing is spared.

JEANNINE BROWN, CARLA DAHL AND
WENDY CORBIN REUSCHLING,
BECOMING WHOLE AND HOLY

There is no circumstance, no trouble, no testing, that can ever
touch me until, first of all, it has gone past God and past Christ,
right through to me. If it has come that far, it has come with
great purpose, which I may not understand at the moment.

ALAN REDPATH

⫴

W e've noticed that as people grow older, they tend to move in
one of two directions: either they become sweeter as they age or
they become more cantankerous. They become wiser and more
like Jesus, or they become bitter and more like the worst versions

of themselves. This happens because life is formation. All that we do and experience shapes us in one direction or another, primarily based on how we respond to what happens to us and the experiences of everyday life—both extraordinary and mundane.

The same holds true for the ministry of eldership. We have seen leaders emerge from similar trials having grown and become more Christlike or having become dejected and ready to quit. The difference seems to be where we see God in the midst of our ministry struggles, either absent or present, and the questions we ask about those struggles. Some ask, "God, why is this happening to me/us?" Others choose a different course: "God, what can you form in me/us through this?" Both views of God form us, as will both kinds of questions, but they form us in very different directions.

The sin most prevalent in church leadership is a fixation on numbers and results, and a corresponding inattention to the state of our own souls. Even more, there's an inattention to how those numbers and results—how ministry itself—are forming and shaping us. For that reason, we believe we should stop trying so hard to develop our ministries and start realizing that our ministries are developing us. How we face the realities of church leadership will be a determining factor not just in what our church becomes, but also in what we become. Leadership and ministry will form us. The only question is, into what?

How Does God Form Us in Ministry?

Some are hesitant to take on an elder role because, by doing so, they open themselves to the scrutiny and occasionally the criticism of others. As a young leader, I (Bob) absolutely hated the fishbowl effect of ministry—that everyone was watching me closely and my mistakes appeared to count for so much more than the mistakes of others. It seemed profoundly unfair to my young mind that personal shortcomings, which would never even be an issue in terms of most people's employment, could easily cost me my job, my reputation and my community. Never mind that maybe the reason it bothered me so much was that I had a surplus of those shortcomings.

Through years of living in the unfailing eye of critics and cranks, I've come to see the fishbowl in a slightly different light. It is now something I gladly embrace.

Richard Baxter, a Puritan pastor in the 1600s, spoke of this church leadership life this way:

> While you are as lights set upon a hill, think not to lie hid. Take heed therefore to yourselves, and do your work as those that remember that the world looks on them, and that with the quick-sighted eye of malice, ready to make the worst of all, to find the smallest fault where it is, to aggravate it where they find it, to divulge it and to take advantage of it to their own designs, and to make faults where they cannot find them. How cautiously, then, should we walk before so many ill-minded observers![1]

Baxter understood that those who call others to live like Jesus will necessarily be faulted when failing to live so themselves. He encourages us to live as though the world is watching—because it is. There are those in our lives ready who shout "hypocrite!" at the slightest provocation, who call us out for human failings that they themselves share and even, as Baxter says, create faults when they cannot find them.

But Baxter took it further, saying we ought to be glad for this.

> As you take yourselves for the lights of the churches, you may expect that men's eyes will be upon you. If other men may sin without observation, so cannot you. And you should thankfully consider how great a mercy this is, that you have

so many eyes to watch over you, and so many ready to tell you of your faults; and thus have greater helps than others, at least for restraining you from sin. Though they may do it with a malicious mind, yet you have the advantage of it.[2]

The fact that you as an elder have more eyes on you and more people examining how you live means you have greater helps in living right and avoiding sin. What some mean for evil, God means for your good; what seems like a downside of ministry is actually a means of maturation, of formation. Practically speaking, this life-lived-before-others pushes us to do what we know we ought to do. It often keeps us from falling into things we might fall into were we not being watched so closely.

Let's be clear though: it's not enough. We all know that what we are after is character and heart change, but the structure in which we are living before a watching church and a watching world can help us form the habits and rhythms of holiness we so desire.

As we try to find the heart of Christ and his character formed ever more within us, we have the advantage of knowing that there are many eyes around us to "encourage" us to keep to the straight and narrow. My (Bob's) sense is that those who embrace this find that, over time, what starts as external becomes more and more internal. Slowly we realize that what we choose to do or not do because others are watching becomes a matter of true character through habit. Because I know others are watching, I think twice about what I say publicly, what I look at in the checkout line of the supermarket and how I speak to my kids in church or out on the street in front of my neighbors. More and more, those choices become a part of who I am. This is especially true when I choose to see those moments of choice as *kairos* moments,[3] occasions when God is breaking in, using my awareness of a watching world to communicate to me about the character he wants to see formed in me.

But what if we fail to embrace this? What of those who are shipwrecked by moral failure, character deficiencies and private sins made public? Those who chafe at the idea of the fishbowl of ministry and the Christian life often find themselves living one way in public and another in private. It's as though anger at the scrutiny leads them to a divided life, one where they are willing to play by the rules in public but insist on their own rules in private. Frustration with the audience around them that seems so eager to find fault leads them to ignore the true Audience. And as we know from watching others flame out in spectacular crash-and-burns, the impact is often horrendous. Families, churches and the reputation of the church as a whole are damaged significantly.

Elders, make peace with the fishbowl. It will be there whether you accept it or not. By embracing it, you might find yourself spurred on to the love and good deeds to which you aspire, and you might avoid the sins that have brought down so many in ministry. Again, as Baxter writes, "You should thankfully consider how great a mercy this is, that you have so many eyes to watch over you."[4] Let the Holy Spirit use the public life you lead to shape and form you.

SELF-DIFFERENTIATION

One of the primary differences between those who make it for the long haul in leading and ministering to others and those who don't is the level of self-differentiation they are able to achieve. Self-differentiation is the ability to separate one's intellectual or emotional functioning from that of family or other groups. In other words, it is the ability to know who you are without reference to who others believe you to be. This happens when your identity is rooted in something other than the transitory—your job or title, the esteem with which others hold you or the way you feel about your current performance. For the Christian leader, self-differentiation depends on our view of ourselves as the beloved of God, children of a God who cares for us because of who we are and accepts us because of what Christ has done.

Leading in a church setting is especially challenging for our self-differentiation. We're often expected to respond not just to the needs but also to the wants and preferences of a very diverse community at all stages of spiritual development. We're looked up to by some and looked down on by others; we're seen as the solution by some and the problem by others. In all of this, we're dealing with our own spiritual development and with our identity as leaders and members of the very communities we're also trying to lead. Trying to be "all things to all people" is a sound missiological principle, but doing so without first having a grounded core identity—dependent not on what people think of us but on what God thinks of us—will quickly have us running in twelve different directions at once and losing our mission orientation. "Doing God's will means at times resisting the loving appeal of nervous friends who offer us another, safer agenda"[5]—or resisting the nervous preferences of our community or fellow leaders.

Three things have been invaluable to me in my quest to be the leader God means me to be.

1. Knowing the difference between **to** *and* **for.** Elders face a constant temptation to feel responsible for their community, their spiritual well-being, their marriages and their continued presence and involvement with their community. The problem is that as a community grows, as more and more marriages struggle (and perhaps fail) and as some decide to walk away from your church (and even the faith), that weight on your shoulders increases exponentially. Feeling responsible for others when we have no control over their behavior quickly leads to leaders who either try to control the behavior through whatever means necessary or who burn out under the load.

The good news is that you are not responsible *for* anyone in your community. As an elder, you have responsibilities *to* them. You have the responsibility to love them, to teach them, to carefully and lovingly correct and exhort and encourage them, but you are not responsible for what they choose to do with that. Your responsibility includes doing all you can to point them to Jesus, but it puts the results firmly in their choices and the work of the Holy Spirit.

The same holds true with the overall community. We tend to take responsibility both when things are going well and when they aren't, when we're growing and when things feel stagnant and dead. In both, we overestimate both our influence and our responsibility. As leaders, we don't make the church grow—God does. Our responsibility is to discharge our duties faithfully as elders and then leave the results up to God. We are responsible to our communities to be the best leaders we can be, to offer the best we can in terms of spurring others on toward love and good deeds and sounding a clear call to be the church Jesus had in mind. Ultimately, God is responsible for his church and its members, not us. The outcomes of our efforts rest in his hands, not on our shoulders.

2. The place of the disciplines. While acknowledging no community is perfectly mature, we would contend that the reason more communities are not more spiritually mature is because their leaders are not more spiritually mature. Why aren't they? As Dallas Willard points out in *The Spirit of the Disciplines,* while we want to react as Christ would react, behave as Christ would behave and lead as Christ would lead, we are unwilling to do the things and practice the disciplines that enabled him to react, behave and lead as he did. Willard writes, "We must learn to follow his preparations, the disciplines for life in God's rule that enabled him to receive his Father's constant and effective support while doing his will."[6] Programs and teaching series will not do half as much good in a community as elders who transparently live their lives and their practices before a watching community.

Disciplines for God. Many times I have sat with both pastors and elders who spoke of being spiritually dry. What I hear over and over again is that it's difficult to find or make the time for reading Scripture; it's hard to pray in a disciplined and consistent manner; and it's nearly impossible to set aside time simply to sit and be present to God in the midst of the busyness and rigors of life, work and ministry.

When I was a youth pastor, one day I sat at my desk, staring down at my open Bible and wondering, *Would I do this if I thought no one would ever ask me if I had?* At the time, my truthful answer was no. It was then I realized I needed a major paradigm shift in how I related to God. Leadership demanded that I engage with the spiritual disciplines, but leadership was not sufficient to make those practices vital and real in my life. What I needed was to fall in love with God again—to see in him a loveliness and a value apart from how he contributed to my position in church leadership. Leadership will "call the question" in your life: do you love God for God, or God as a means to an end? To put it another way, are you in love with him or are you seeing relationship with him as a necessary means to maintaining leadership and your reputation?

Disciplines for others. One of the main reasons leaders find it so hard to be disciplined in spending time in God's Word, solitude and stillness, prayer, meditation and fasting is that they feel they are so busy with life, so busy in doing good, so busy serving God and the community that they neglect the care of their own souls. As Baxter says, they are busy preparing meals for others even while they themselves are starving. You simply can't feed anyone without having been fed yourself. What you offer to others will be of little nutritional value to them unless it flows from a vital, connected, disciplined relationship with God.

This can be particularly difficult for elders who are not in paid ministry. There is a temptation to see serving the church in leadership, attending meetings and fulfilling all the obligations of an elder as, if not sufficient for our spiritual lives, all that we really have the bandwidth to do.

When talking with pastors and other ministry leaders, I urge them to see their own spiritual formation as a way of not simply growing in relationship with the God who loves them, but also of loving others around them. My wife, my children and the people in my church need me to be in prayer and in Scripture regularly, in solitude and silence often. They need me to be grounded spiritually and growing, because that's the only way I'll ever be able to discharge my responsibilities to them faithfully. Seeing what we do publicly as loving service to our community is only half the story. Seeing what we do privately as we care for our souls also as loving service to others is the rest.

Disciplines for ourselves. The late-night phone calls, the inevitable conflicts, the difficulty of seeing others make wrong choices—all of these have an impact. Practicing the disciplines helps shape that impact for our good.

> Implementing the spiritual disciplines in our lives also helps us minimize our anxious reactivity and choose a more constructive response instead. For example, the practice of studying the Scriptures brings the cognitive perspective to an emotionally laden situation. We are reminded by the words on the page to love our enemy when our natural reaction is to lash out in hatred. As we pray for our enemy, we open ourselves up to consider compassion and mercy. As we confess our sins, we face our sinfulness and avoid over-focusing on the sinfulness of the other. Gradually, we experience transformation, becoming the kind of people who are actually capable of forgiving an enemy.[7]

How do some handle the stress of leadership and life so they grow from it while others feel more and more like burned-out husks, stumbling through another meeting, dealing with another crisis? We would venture to say it comes down to how they view themselves and those stresses. Spending time with God reminds us of his presence, even in the most difficult parts of life and church leadership. It grounds us in the character of Christ and informs our reactions. It enables us to choose loving responses rather than react or be defensive. And it reminds us that even in the hardest parts of leading a church community, God wants to use what we go through and our responses to it to form and shape us and our communities.

3. *Believing the gospel.* A number of years into church leadership, I found I was having great difficulty sleeping. I could get to sleep just fine. In fact, I was often so exhausted I would be out cold minutes after my head hit the pillow. My problem was that somewhere in the middle of the night, I would wake up, and my mind would begin racing with thoughts of church—what needed to get done, who needed to be taken care of, how we were doing, how I was doing as a pastor. Sunday nights were especially difficult as I replayed that morning's gathering, thinking of the visitors I was sure were not adequately greeted, the lack in our children's programs and especially my sermon—always my sermon. I would lie there reliving jokes that went flat, parts I missed or messed up, and the seeming lack of response from the congregation.

Many was the Sunday night that I would think, *Well, that's it. No one is coming back after that performance.* When someone left our church, I had more sleepless nights. When someone criticized my pastoring, yet more. Leadership was having a very forming effect on my soul, but not a positive one. Some of our elders have struggled at times with similar feelings, though perhaps not to the same degree. There's no doubt that when you accept leadership in a community, the struggles of that community and those within it can overwhelm you.

I longed—and prayed for—rest and peace, and God answered me. I realized that though I said my Savior was Jesus, I was actually relying on my people's approval. In a moment of raw honesty, I had to admit that *they* had become my savior. When I felt like things were going well and my performance was approved of, I was elated. When it went the other way, I struggled with dejection, insomnia and even depression. Slowly I began to realize that my real need wasn't just for physical rest, but for something much deeper: what the writer of Hebrews calls "a Sabbath-rest for the people of God; for anyone who enters God's rest also rests from his own work, just as God did from his" (Hebrews 4:9-10).

God began to speak to me about my striving, about my sorry attempts at self-justification and my desire to prove my worth and value—my efforts to save myself through my performance as a church leader. Rest is what I needed, but not just the rest of my body in sleep and not even the rest of my mind from the cares and worries of ministry. On a deeper, more significant level, what I needed was the Sabbath rest of my soul in the finished work of Jesus.

What we do as elders and pastors matters. It's vitally important work, and we want to do it well, but we need to want to do it well for the right reasons. We need to make sure we do it so that people will see, love and esteem the person of Jesus, not us. We need to do it so that people will lay down their false gods and embrace the One who can save them.

In the midst of all of that, we want to avoid preaching a different message with our lives than we do with our mouths. We want to avoid modeling a message of self-salvation. As we lean back on Christ in both the exciting times and the hard times and learn to rest in him and what he has done for us, slowly but surely, our minds become calmer and our bodies more at peace.

As elders, we are called to ministry and to preaching the good news that God himself has come to rescue and redeem us through the work of Jesus on our behalf—and that nothing else can or will save us. We must also realize the person we need to preach it to most often: ourselves.

ENSURING SPIRITUAL FORMATION, NOT MALFORMATION

So how do we ensure that ministry is forming us more into the image of Christ and not less? By remaining mindful of our self-differentiation, our identity in Christ that is rooted not in what people think of us as leaders but in what God thinks of us as his beloved children. We do so by faithfully discharging our duties to our communities without crossing over into feeling responsible for them, and so unwittingly carrying the weight of results that rightly belongs on the shoulders of the Holy Spirit alone. We do this by practicing the classic Christian disciplines out of love for God and others, and for the sake of our souls. And we do so by believing the gospel we preach—that it is Jesus who saves us, not our performance, the growth of our church, the applause of people or anything else. We rest the weight of souls firmly on him.

In addition, as you navigate some of the harder tasks of ministry, stop often and examine your motivations, particularly when you are tempted to do things the easy or the expedient way. Do things the hard way. Do what scares you. If you are tempted to answer a criticism, do so in person or with a phone call, not with an email. Why? Not simply because you might get better results, but because doing what scares you and facing up to hard conversations can have a much more forming effect on you, creating a boldness and a trust in God that a simple email might not lead to. Evaluate every decision, both individually and corporately, with the questions "What will this form in us?" "What spiritual impact will this have on our community?" and "Is this a means to growth in faith and depending on God or a shortcut so we don't have to?"

Recognize that the hard things are often the best things. We all know we grow more in times of struggle than in times when things are going well. We need to embrace this on a leadership level as well as a personal one. Can you thank God for the tough times in the life of your community—or at least for what he has done in those tough times? Can you learn to look at trials and tribulation, if not with joy, as James encourages us, then at least with a view that God can use those trials for your maturing?

In ministry and in life, everything is formation—if we will treat it as such.

8

Team Leadership

*An emotionally healthy approach to leadership is polycentric.
Within such a community we learn both to lead and follow,
to share our brokenness and victories, and to help each
other mature in Christ for his honor and glory.*

JR WOODWARD, *CREATING A MISSIONAL CULTURE*

*The answer, we discovered, was trust—submitting ourselves
to each other in love and vulnerability. We learned to trust
that the Spirit speaks and works not just in each person
individually but in His church. We learned to test our
agendas, preferences, opinions and sensitivities based on
giftings of the Holy Spirit. Through the discipline of mutual
submission we found ourselves becoming the kinds of people
who increasingly trusted the Holy Spirit and each other.*

DAVID FITCH

During the first few years of our church life, I (Bob) felt very alone in ministry. Though there were others with me in giving to and serving our church community, I felt like I was bearing the weight of leadership largely on my own. It wasn't until a few years later that I realized, with extreme gratitude, that it didn't need to be so. God had given me a built-in support team to bear the load and to share the joys and the challenges of the work of church: my elder team.

Leading as a Community Within a Community

As leaders, we are not leading as much as we are providing an example to those in our church. One of the places where this most often breaks down is in how we provide examples of interdependence and community. Too many pastors go it alone, finding support outside their church community as they struggle largely on their own with the work of ministry. They use their elder teams as more of an advisory board to approve or modify leadership decisions.

We want to propose a different model: the community within a community. Whenever eldership is spoken of in Scripture, it's in terms of a plurality. We see elders (plural) being appointed (Acts 14:23), making decisions and formulating "policy" together (Acts 15:6), being spoken of as a group (Acts 20:17; 21:18; Philippians 1:1) and praying for and laying hands on others to appoint them to minister to the church (1 Timothy 4:14; James 5:14). Some churches, whether through denominational polity or because they are new, have only one elder: the senior or lead pastor. This is not the model that the New Testament, or the rest of Scripture, points us to. Every pastor should listen well to the question Moses' father-in-law, Jethro, asked him: "What are you really accomplishing here? Why are you trying to do this all alone?" (paraphrase; see Exodus 18:14-23). Jethro then gave him some wise advice: "You and these people who come to you will only wear yourselves out. The work is too heavy for you; you cannot handle it alone" (v. 18). On hearing that, Moses appointed others to help in the task of leading and judging the community of Israel.

Shared leadership is a common theme in Scripture. While nowhere does the New Testament give a prescribed number of elders for each church, it makes it clear that the number should be greater than one. Local churches should have a plurality of eldership. But having a number of elders doesn't change much if all those elders do is rubber-stamp pastoral decisions or leave the work of ministry to the pastor. There must be shared responsibility and work, shared joy and struggle—in a word, community.

The elder team should function as a small model of what the larger church ought to be, bearing each other's burdens, praying together, challenging and teaching one another, forgiving each other. The elder team ought to be listening to God together and discerning what they are hearing for themselves, each other and the community, not simply waiting for the lead person to come back from the mountain with a new direction or program for them to approve (or more often in dysfunctional churches, veto). They ought to take seriously all relational breaks or friction on the team. They ought to love one another and love being together, and if that's not the case, they ought to figure out why and resolve it.

Many elder teams function like a golf foursome; they play the same course together, but each one is essentially playing his or her own game. We encourage you to see leadership as being more like a football or baseball team. Each person plays within a specific role that supports and enhances others—playing, winning and losing together as a team.

This plurality—or community within a community—requires a number of shifts in our thinking.

FROM LEAD PASTOR TO TEAM

Who's really in charge of your church community—that is, under the leadership of Christ, where does the final decision-making authority rest? Does the buck stop at the pastor's desk? Or does it stop with the elder team? That's a critical distinction that will have different practical outworkings. In the former, a senior pastor makes executive decisions and then expects to be backed up by the elders should the outcome prove negative, which is the expectation in a corporate board context. In the latter, a team is heavily invested in what happens and needs time and prayer to process before most mission-critical decisions are made, which is what we see modeled over and over again in the New Testament.

The shift from one to the other isn't always easy. Our churches have been conditioned to look to one person as having the final say (the CEO model taken from the business world). They expect that the main speaking voice on Sundays will be the one who is leading them. Never mind that Scripture nowhere points to such a model.

Having a biblical plurality in leadership requires that we talk about, teach on and exercise authority differently. The community must know that a team of coequals is leading them. Even if one person is identified as a lead pastor (because of his or her full-time role or leadership giftings), care should be taken to emphasize that though that person may have an organizing, leading role on the team, he or she is first among equals, not simply first.

FROM BOARD MEMBER TO TEAM EQUIPPER

Earlier we mentioned that it's important what you call elders, and we discouraged the use of "elder board." Further, we don't believe that the primary role of elders is making decisions for the church. Certainly, that is a part of the role, but not the most essential part. Elders are individuals called out from within the community for the good of and the equipping of the community.

To do this, they must first be invested in the position of elder, not seeing it as a once- or twice-a-month meeting, but as a role they are called to fulfill within the community. Second, they must understand their own giftings and the way those benefit both their smaller community of fellow elders and the larger community. And third, they must be willing to help identify others in the community who share those same gifts and then take part in equipping them to use those gifts for the good of the community and the world.

In Ephesians 4, we clearly see this dynamic described in Scripture. Paul wrote, "Now these are the gifts Christ gave to the church: the apostles, the prophets, the evangelists, and the pastors and teachers. Their responsibility is to equip God's people to do his work and build up the church, the body of Christ" (vv. 11-12 NLT).

Paul's intention here is not to provide another gifts list, as in other places where he describes the Holy Spirit empowerments given to believers. Here he describes foundational gifts given to the church as a whole, and those gifts are specific people: apostles, prophets, evangelists, shepherds[1] and teachers. These people have a specific role within the community: equipping others and building up the body, all focused toward the maturity and unity of that diverse body. One chapter later in Ephesians 5, in the midst of a discussion on life in such a community, Paul gave a command that proves especially important, not just in community life, but in leadership teams: "Submit to one another" (v. 21).

We believe that the gifts mentioned here constitute a type of spiritual leadership DNA for our communities. These people are given to our churches for equipping toward mission and maturity, and as such, they ought to be an integral part of the leadership makeup in any local community. As JR Woodward writes in *Creating a Missional Culture*, "I propose that the church ought to be led by a Spirit-gifted polycentric team of apostles, prophets, evangelists, pastors and teachers who model and equip their fellow priests in the communal way of life patterned after our Triune God. Then we can more fully follow Christ into the world for the sake of the world, by the power of the Holy Spirit, where we seek to join God in the renewal of all things."[2]

DIVERSE LEADERSHIP, MULTIPLICITY OF GIFTS

Alan Hirsch and Michael Frost point out in their seminal work, *The Shaping of Things to Come*, that the modern church has grown comfortable with shepherd/pastors and teachers, but tends not to know what to do with apostles, prophets and evangelists. These types are generally not invited into church leadership and often make their way into parachurch ministries, where they can more fully exercise their giftings.

The cost of this to the church as a whole has been huge. The apostles are out pioneering new works and organizations, the prophets are leading justice ministries and largely speaking to the church from the margins, and the evangelists are forced to form their own organizations to reach campuses and cities for Christ. All the while, churches complain that these parachurch leaders are sucking resources and people out of the local church. There's an easy way to solve this. We need to take seriously the Ephesians 4 model: church leaders make room for all of these foundational gifts on elder and leadership teams. In this way we provide a well-rounded leadership team that is set free to equip an increasingly well-rounded church.

When churches have one person at the top of their organizational chart, with one type of gift, it tends to flavor the whole ministry of that church.

- Churches with a strong teacher at the top tend to be intellectual, knowledge-based communities where doctrine is seen to be of utmost importance. In these communities, spirituality can easily be equated with Scripture study and knowledge.

- Churches led by strong pastoral/shepherding types tend to do well at loving each other and caring for the needs of the body. In these communities, spirituality is equated with love and the "one anothers" of the New Testament.

- Churches with strong prophetic voices in charge tend to speak truth to power and do well at justice-oriented ministry. In these churches, spirituality is equated with care for the poor, the marginalized and the outsider.

- Churches with evangelists as the lead pastor tend to be characterized by a heart for those who don't know Jesus and have a strong emphasis on evangelism. In these churches, spirituality is equated with a heart for the lost and telling others about Jesus.

- And churches with a strong apostolic personality at the fore tend to break new ground, constantly pushing the bounds of creativity in ministry and forging ahead into new territory as a church. In these communities, spirituality tends to be experienced as something new every other month.

But imagine a church led collectively by a team in which all these gifts are represented—where all the concerns brought by a balanced, mutually submissive group of apostles, evangelists, prophets, shepherds and teachers are considered and factored into the life of the community. Pushed by their apostolic leaders to break new ground, they would be innovative and willing to take risks.

Brought back consistently to their core values and the heart of God by their prophetic leaders, they would stay centered and true to their calling as a church. Reminded constantly of God's heart for people who don't know Jesus, they would continually evaluate what they do and say as a community, asking, "How will non-Christians hear this?" They would find themselves more and more drawn outward to their non-Christian neighbors and to creating a place where those neighbors, friends and coworkers could belong even before they believe and to journeying with them toward Jesus.

Drawn inward by shepherding leaders, they would grow in their care and concern for others in the body and in their ability to minister to one another. And resourced by teaching leaders, they would more fully understand God's heart as revealed in Scripture and what the way of Jesus looks like in our time and place.

APEST: THE FIVE GIFTINGS IN ACTION

Let's consider these giftings more in depth.

The apostle. The word *apostle* means "messenger" or "sent one." In ancient Greece, the word *apostolos* was a nautical term used to describe the lead ship within a fleet that had been sent out on a mission. It was seen as the representative or ambassador sent on behalf of some other authority.

In Scripture the term *apostle* refers not so much to a title, but to a characteristic. The apostles were the ones sent to other places to tell people about Jesus. They were the pioneers taking the message of the gospel into new territory. The original twelve disciples (minus Judas) became apostles. Jesus sent them out after adding Matthias to their ranks to replace Judas (Acts 1:21-26). They were soon joined by others, like Barnabas, sent out by the church and called apostles.

When we talk about an apostolic gifting, we're referring to a God-given impulse and gifting to take the gospel and the work of the church into new territories or new methodologies. Many missionaries have this apostolic gifting, but so do many entrepreneurs; they see a need and have a near-irresistible impulse to meet it. Apostles see a need and desire to bring the Holy Spirit and the body of Christ into it. These spiritual entrepreneurs and kingdom trail-blazers have a high tolerance for risk. They are strategists, innovators and visionaries who are willing to step up and go to places nobody has gone before and try things nobody has tried before.

In our experience, many church planters have this apostolic gift. There's a holy discontent with church as normal. They long to see communities created that can fill the gap and reach out to those not currently being reached by other churches. Apostles feel closest to God when they are stepping out in faith, taking big risks for the kingdom.

The prophet. We have often found a great amount of cultural baggage and misunderstanding surrounding this term. Set aside your ideas of the prophet as one who speaks direct words from God unerringly. The New Testament idea of prophecy includes both the foretelling aspect, but also a more general "forthtelling" aspect of revealing the heart of God. Those with the gift of prophecy won't necessarily be able to tell you who will win the World Series, but they might have God-given insight into your sports addiction and what God might like to address regarding the issue. In community, the prophets are the ones who call us back to foundational things. They sense when we are straying off our mission; they feel strongly when we are not living up to our potential communally; and they speak into the life of others and the community. Prophets often have an intense bent toward issues related to the poor and disenfranchised and help local churches to see where the church can be involved with justice, which matters significantly to God.

Prophets can also be extremely sensitive to the promptings of the Spirit. They have a naturally supernatural posture and are often willing to press in to issues others ignore. They recognize and can connect the dots of God's work in people's lives that others may not discern. They can be questioners, agitators and provocateurs stirring up the waters of the status quo. Though it may make some people uncomfortable, prophets remind us that the Spirit is still actively speaking and working and that we would be wise not only to listen but also to anticipate God speaking to us.

Interestingly, in my experience, prophets are often, though not always, introverts who find God in the quiet, solitary spaces of contemplation. They are good at listening to God and responding appropriately, and they desire that their community do the same.

The evangelist. While all Christians are called to share the gospel, for some this seems to be second nature. While many of us might struggle to build natural and trusting relationships with non-Christians, there is nothing evangelists enjoy more. They are especially wired, not in bringing God into every conversation, but in seeing where he's already at work and helping others do the same. They tend to be able to strike up conversations with people about faith issues in a way that even strangers feel valued, appreciated and engaged in significant conversation. In their *The Forgotten Ways Handbook*, Alan Hirsch and Darryn Altclass write, "Maybe it's more helpful to view evangelism as uncovering the God who is already present in their lives. In this sense, evangelism would be focused on evoking the memory of God and would consist of probing, prodding, and asking insightful questions."[3]

Further, they are passionate about seeing their church community connect with people who don't know Jesus, and they tend to look at everything a church does through the eyes of their latest non-Christian friend. Elders who are evangelists regularly bring up questions such as "What are we doing to raise the temperature on cultivating spiritual friendship with those outside our church?" and "How are we spending our time and energy out in the community and not just in our church?" These questions continually remind us of the importance of pushing out to be near the people Jesus loves dearly. Evangelists feel most excited and connected with God when they are cooperating with God in seeing people move closer to Jesus. Not only are they recruiters to the work of the kingdom, they also push the church out into the world, refusing to let the church remain inwardly focused.

The shepherd/pastor. If the apostle helps to catalyze the mission, the shepherd/pastor works to humanize the church. The shepherd is the one who notices when people aren't doing well or who has insight into what would be particularly helpful for a certain group. They care—and care deeply. They feel the weight of the failing marriages, the sick and the struggling, and they long to see the church as a whole respond well to needs. Their hearts break when they see needy or wounded people struggling, and they frequently shed tears over their condition.

Because shepherds are caregivers, they are often drawn to helping professions. These folks continually advocate that the church not forget about anyone, not leave anyone behind, but respond thoroughly and compassionately in every situation. Conversely, they can wear themselves out caring for others, and special care should be given to them to make sure they are engaging in self-care and being looked after by others. Shepherds find God in community; they love to be around people. Because of this, people easily trust them, knowing they will be heard, respected and loved.

The teacher. Teachers love the Scriptures and love seeing God's Word translated and communicated in a systematized and clear way that is easily understood. To them, it matters deeply what Scriptures say, and therefore it matters that a community grow in its knowledge of it. An immature teacher is likely to be always trying to correct a fine point of doctrine from last week's sermon, while a mature teacher is concerned with the overall direction of a community's learning, making sure it is pointed in the direction of the heart of God. Teachers ignite people to a deeper level of scriptural engagement. Few things light the fire of spiritually gifted teachers more than seeing people have "aha" moments when reading and studying Scripture and seeing how it applies to their lives.

There are both mature and immature expressions of all these gifts. Part of the leadership task is to help others to move from immature expressions (the apostle who gives people whiplash by changing strategy or direction constantly, the prophet who speaks dogmatically without submitting insights to the team or the community for feedback, the teacher who becomes convinced that she has it right and everyone around her has it wrong) to a more mature, body-building expression of their gift.[4]

HOW DOES TEAM LEADERSHIP WORK?

What does all this look like? A polycentric elder team meeting looks more like an intense conversation between friends and less like a board meeting. There may or may not be an official agenda, and everyone's input is wanted and expected on whatever is discussed. There aren't many votes; consensus is sought, in the context of submitting to one another. Issues are looked at with a multiperspective posture—that is, each member of the team helps the others to see issues from the vantage point of their particular gifting.

In our (Bob's) community, I have always tended to carry the apostolic initiative. Generally, when our elders weren't working through a problem or talking about how to do something better, I was proposing something new. I often think about new ways of approaching something, new initiatives inside or outside our church community, and I would be bursting with energy to bring them to the rest of the team so I could hear them tell me what amazing ideas they were and how they should be implemented tomorrow.

At that point, one of the prophetic voices on our team would speak up and ask questions like "How does this fit the values of our community? Where does that fit into our mission?" The evangelist among us would ask, "How will this impact those in our community who don't yet know Jesus? Will this turn them off or away? Will it make sense to them?" The shepherds on the team would want to know how we would care for people through whatever paradigm shift I was proposing, often mentioning specific names. And the teacher would wonder what the biblical basis was and how we would craft language to explain such a thing.

Sometimes I would see that my idea was just that—my idea. It was not really a God-given inspiration, but rather something I thought would be cool. But other times it was through discussions like these, as we all mulled over an idea from these different perspectives, we began to sense the voice of God and to see new possibilities for our community.

Often someone else would have the great idea, much in line with who they were on our team and their gifting: how to be more open and accessible as a community to nonbelievers; how to care for new Christians, couples in crisis or the sick; a sermon series that would be helpful for our community in dealing with whatever we happened to be dealing with at the time.

At the beginning of our church venture, before we had a filled-out elder team, I as the church planter had to wear more than just the apostolic hat. I had to be the prophetic voice, the main teacher of the community, the one looking after everyone and the one asking, "How are we doing at reaching people for Christ?" As the team grew and as more elders identified their giftings, I was able to hand off those roles. I gave up running the teaching calendar of the church and being the main preaching voice to a staff elder who had the passion and giftings to do those things. I looked to others to be the main prophetic voices in our team and to our church, not because I didn't see some of the same things they did in our community, but because they often saw them more clearly and could speak more directly about them. We invited one person onto the team in particular, not just because we saw him as a qualified elder, but because we knew he was at heart an evangelist, something that was missing from our team at that point.

In each case, as we identified the giftings of a particular elder, either before or shortly after he came on the team, I felt a weight lift from my shoulders. Eventually I gave up the title of lead pastor, not because I didn't want it, but because it no longer applied. We had moved from me leading the team to the team leading itself as a community within a community.

One thing you'll discover as you begin to identify the giftings on your team is that there may be a hole somewhere. Perhaps there isn't a prophetic voice or someone passionate about and gifted for evangelism. That's when you begin to pray as a team that God will raise up that leader in your community and that you together will recognize that person. Or you look at someone who is possibly elder material and definitely gifted in the area you need and begin asking, "What could we do to prepare him for eldership? What kind of track can we put him on that will prepare him for this role?"

Another thing you may discover is that someone's primary gifting isn't as needed on your team as much as her secondary gifting is. One of our former elders, Sarah, is a shepherd at heart. Her blog was titled "I Like You!" Sarah cares deeply for people, and it shows. When she came to our team, we had a number of shepherding gifts represented. But what we didn't have was a prophetic voice, someone who would hold our feet to the fire over our stated core values and goals, someone who would ask (especially me as the lead pastor) the hard questions about where we were and where we were going as a community.

Luckily for us, that was Sarah's secondary gifting, and she became a strong prophetic voice on our team, challenging us to care more for the poor, to be involved in other countries, to think through whether the latest greatest idea I had was really a good direction for our community. Though some pastors would chafe at such a voice on their elder team, I loved it. It grounded me. It helped me shape my apostolic vision into something real and practical for our church.

And lest you think such a combination must necessarily lead to an oppositional dynamic, let me assure you that Sarah has always been one of my staunchest defenders, and even when she was shooting down my ideas, I appreciated her heart for our community and her wisdom.

There are two main concerns that keep some from embracing a team approach to leadership:

1. Personal: our egos as leaders keep us from ceding power and authority to others.

2. Communal: we genuinely worry that giving over leadership to those who may not have the same seminary training or pastoral experience as we do might negatively impact the church.

The first is hard for us to admit: we *like* authority and calling the shots. We didn't get into ministry for the accolades, but we sure don't mind them. Many gifted leaders are hesitant to give place to others of equal or greater giftings. The challenge we face is the same one faced by John the Baptist: seeing ourselves decrease that others might increase. We allow others to do the things God has gifted them to do so that we might focus on the things that God has gifted us to do as well as devote time to equipping others with giftings similar to ours.

The second is a genuine concern. Truthfully, the reason more pastors don't share the pulpit is that few in their congregations have the preaching training and experience they have. The problem is, this becomes a self-perpetuating cycle. If someone has to preach at the same or only slightly lower level than the lead pastor to get a shot at preaching, the community will never develop preachers. And we could say the same about a lot of other ministries that have begun to fall under the category of "professional" ministry.

There are people in your church that God has gifted and called to do specific ministries within your community. But they'll never develop those gifts unless someone gives them a chance. That means bringing others along with you as you do ministry, sharing your vision for that particular area, helping them as they develop their skills and then releasing them to do it. They won't do it the way you would. But that's part of the beauty of diversity in the body. They may not do it up to your standards of excellence. But that's the "tax" a community pays to develop people. Whenever we have someone take their first turn in the pulpit on a Sunday morning, we have visitors who never come back. I've made peace with that. It's a price my community and I are willing to pay to see men and women develop their gifts of leading the whole community through a passage of Scripture.

The elder who's been given control of the preaching calendar doesn't do it the same way or work through Scripture exactly as I would. And that's okay, because I am trusting that God is at work in him as he prayerfully considers where our community needs to go scripturally and as he listens to input from the elders and formulates the teaching calendar. Some things I've been happy to hand off, but some things I have given away with clenched teeth, because I loved to do them. But in both cases, I have done so with trust that God was leading our community. The ultimate pastor of our church is Jesus, and he's still working, still gifting and leading, and still growing us toward maturity.

In the final consideration, a polycentric team approach to leadership will protect both you as a leader and your church. Plurality eliminates temptation in the mind of a sole/primary pastor to abuse or assume too much power or to have too little accountability. Too much power in the hands of a single leader can be costly and damaging. Leadership centered primarily on one person in a religious setting is a characteristic of cults, not of a healthy church.[5]

Simply put, each local church needs more than one elder. Since Christ is the head of the church, it is important that we do not promote a hierarchal, top-down, commander-in-chief position of senior pastor. Pastors and elders should work hard to make sure the structure of a church does not depend entirely on one leader. Such structures stray from the principles found in the New Testament and suggest a model of pastor as CEO, rather than a model of a healthy, biblical microcommunity.

Having multiple elders certainly doesn't guarantee a healthy church, but it does position a church well for mission by providing the best opportunity for health to be present. A plurality of elders and a focus on mutual submission between them has several benefits. In addition to accountability, it brings balance and allows for multiple gifts to be expressed and utilized for equipping the body. It embodies the New Testament approach and models unity and mutual submission to the church as a whole. When attacks, accusations, discouraging communications and criticism come from people within a congregation, they can be deflected, carried and dealt with by several elders, rather than one pastor trying to handle all of them. Finally, it can provide a supportive space for future leaders, elders and pastors to be developed within a church structure.

In his book about missional culture, JR Woodward writes, "[Leadership] structures are not neutral. Structures are theological statements."[6] If we truly want to create mission-oriented churches, we must begin with mission-oriented elder teams.

One person cannot lead a church out into the mission of God in the world, and that was never meant to be the case. From the beginning, God, in drawing us into the community of Christ, has seen fit to rest the leadership of the church in teams. These smaller communities within the community shepherd, teach, pastor, equip and lead their churches out into their neighborhoods as they cooperate with God in the rescue and renewal of the world.

9

The Role of Elders in Decision Making

*For the sincere Christian who is committed to
glorifying God through wise decisions, one further
question begs to be answered: How does one get
the requisite wisdom for such decisions?*

<small>GARRY FRIESEN, *DECISION MAKING AND THE WILL OF GOD*</small>

It seemed good to the Holy Spirit and to us.

<small>ACTS 15:28</small>

⫶⫼

When I (Bob) look back at the beginning of our church in
2004, the moments that stand out as significant turning points
all have to do with decisions and discernment. We had a surplus
of the former and a real need for the latter. As we set out to start
a new church community without benefit of a sending church
or a supporting denomination, we knew that we were alone in

many ways. Our dependence on the Holy Spirit to guide and direct our conversations as a community, particularly about where we were going and what we were becoming, became increasingly important.

One of the first questions I remember being asked by our core team as we moved toward planting was "What are you going to do for kids?" (Note well the pronoun *you* in that sentence.) My answer in those days was always the same: "I don't know . . . what are *we* going to do?" Usually there was uncomfortable silence.

Eventually we pushed through that uncomfortable silence into something much better. Those early questions of who would do what and what principles would lie at the core of our community stretched us all to listen not only to the Scriptures and to the Holy Spirit, but also to one another. Because of this, I began to see my role as pastor and elder as one not of solving problems, but of pointing to them, noting the tension around them and allowing the process to work.

Gailyn Van Rheenan says missional churches are "theologically formed, Christ-centered, Spirit-led fellowships that seek faithfully to incarnate the purposes of Christ."[1] As you seek to create and lead a church or to move your existing church increasingly into mission, being Spirit-led must be front and center. Nowhere will that be as important as in the critical area of decision making.

So where does it all begin? The temptation in church leadership (some with the best of intentions, but some with not-so-good intentions) is to see a problem, conceive the solution and set about trying to sell that solution to our congregations. Here we want to propose a different starting point that may sound obvious, but is frequently overlooked.

A central question for us both individually and as a community is this: What do we hear God saying, and what would it look like to respond appropriately? My community attempts to end every Sunday by dialoguing about these questions together as we ask ourselves and each other, "What have we heard the Spirit say through the Word, discussion, prayers, songs and coming to the Table?"

In times of tension, or in times when we sense the Spirit leading us to change, our practice is to call the community to a season of discernment, punctuated by communal times of prayer (which are meant to work hand in hand with individual prayer), discussions and consensus building.

Let's look at the basics and some of the essential practices involved.

THEOLOGICAL RATIONALE

Our goal in these times of discernment is to get to a sense of "it seem[s] good to the Holy Spirit and to us" (Acts 15:28). Much of what Scripture says about discernment has to do with individuals discerning truth from falsehood, but in terms of communal decision making, we can hardly find a better description of the process or the outcome than that of the council of Jerusalem in Acts 15 (see especially v. 28). When faced with the difficult and already divisive issue of integrating Gentiles into the largely Jewish church culture, the apostles went back to Scripture, to reasoned discussion, to prayer and to the role of the Spirit in their midst as they attempted to recognize what God was already doing and to join him in it.

In the same way, our goal as a community is not to come to the most expedient decision or the one that will cause the least amount of controversy. Rather, our desire is to prayerfully walk the community through a dialogue that looks for what God is doing and listens for what God is saying. As Larry Julian writes in his book *God Is My Coach*, "Leaders are so focused on the outcome that they neglect the process—the process of searching God's will."[2] If we discern while leaning heavily on the Spirit and the Word, we can then do our best to formulate an appropriate response. As we do so, we often find ourselves able to say, like the apostles, this course seems like not only the best idea, but also where God himself is leading us.

And, of course, as Leonard Sweet and Frank Viola suggest in their book *Jesus Manifesto*, we want our community, especially in times of discernment and decision making to be "discovering and displaying Christ."[3] If our goal as individuals and as a community is to be a sign and foretaste—that is, a tangible display of what the gospel does in, to and through us—we can think of few better areas to point to the redemptive work of Jesus and the unifying work of the Spirit than in how we move through the difficult waters of decision making in community.

GUIDING THEOLOGICAL THEMES

As we attempt to live out this life in the Spirit communally, here are some of the theological themes and principles that we look to for guidance and that we recommend to you.

The presence of the Holy Spirit in our community. The apostles placed great emphasis on the role of the Spirit in the life of the church in general and in discernment in particular (1 John 2:20-27; 4:1-6). We acknowledge not only the place of the Spirit in our community, but also our radical dependence on him to point us to Jesus and to lead us into places where he is bringing healing and wholeness in the world.

The love of Jesus for our community outweighs our love for our community. As much as we love and want the best for our community, and as much as we may feel we have metaphorically bled for our church, we strive to keep in mind that Christ has literally bled and died for it. His love for and investment in our community is much greater than ours will ever be. Remaining mindful of that fact brings a certain freedom in the face of tough decisions. We can place our community in the hands of the God, who went to such great lengths to make it possible. It's his church. He will build it. We merely join in the process and cooperate as best we can.

The Bible is authoritative. We want to affirm that Scripture is authoritative for the church today. That is, if the person of Jesus is the primary revelation of God to humankind, then Scripture becomes indispensable because it is there that we find not only the narrative of God's redemption (the Old Testament) culminating in the person of Christ (the Gospels), but also the outworking of Christ's work in the new community of the church (the Epistles). Where the Bible speaks, we listen and weigh carefully what it says for our context (Acts 2:42; 2 Timothy 3:14-17).

Leadership is biblical, as is the priesthood of every believer. Though it's a controversial statement in some circles today, the concept of leadership in the church is biblical. Hebrews 13:17 encourages us all to "obey your spiritual leaders, and do what they say. Their work is to watch over your souls, and they are accountable to God" (NLT). First Thessalonians 5:12-13 says, "Dear brothers and sisters, honor those who are your leaders in the Lord's work. They work hard among you and give you spiritual guidance. Show them great respect and wholehearted love because of their work" (NLT).

And yet we also recognize the priesthood of all those in our community who are truly "in Christ" (1 Peter 2:9-10). God does not speak only to and through leaders, so those to whom leadership is entrusted have a responsibility to be good listeners for the voice of God through the mouths and lives of others in the community.

Leadership ought to seek consensus and not lead in a heavy-handed manner. Jesus enjoined his followers to lead in a manner different from those who "lord it over" others (Mark 10:42). When we seek first to be servants of one another, we not only seek for consensus and for opposing and alternative voices to be heard, but

also to do so in a humble and Christlike way, with gentleness
(2 Corinthians 10:1; Colossians 3:12; 1 Timothy 6:11).

THREE KINDS OF DECISIONS

One of the earliest decisions we made together (Bob's community)
was that we would not have formal membership. In those early
days, many believed that the desire to be a place where people
could belong before they believed superseded the need for
formal membership. This meant that we would be—out of
necessity—an elder-led community. Though we would try to
lead by consensus and involve the community as much as
possible, we couldn't do congregational government in the
traditional sense without formal membership. Everyone
understood that and (with a few notable exceptions) have agreed
with and supported the decisions the elders have made.

You may find yourself in a similar elder-led context or perhaps
in a more congregational setting. In either case, we believe that
the following outline of decision types can be a useful tool in the
life of your community. In leading and making decisions directed
toward mission-orientation in a local church context, we work
under the rubric that a particular decision is one of three kinds:

1. Communal: issues put before the community and left up to
   them to decide

2. Elder recommendations: issues the elders have prayed about,
   discussed and believe to be in the best interest of the community, but they still want to build consensus and won't move
   on until that consensus is built

3. Elder decisions: issues the elders, through prayer and discussion, make a decision on and inform the community when
   necessary and appropriate

EXAMPLES

Communal decisions are often related to issues where the entire community is a stakeholder and many potential good decisions or directions exist. For instance, when my church was making the decision to remain in rented, public spaces or to occupy a church-type building, it was left to the community. Also, at one point, we had to make a decision whether to keep a Sunday-evening gathering in southwest Portland going. This decision was put before and left to those who were a part of that gathering. We prayed together, discussed the pros and cons of them folding back into our other gatherings and did our best to make sure everyone felt as though they had been heard. In the end, there was a consensus: though ending those gatherings would be painful, it was the right thing at the right time.

Elder recommendations are things that the elders have prayed through and feel strongly enough about that we want to make a proposal to the community. Some of the proposals could best be summed up by "we won't move unless we feel there's consensus on this" (such as a recent proposal for a community covenant); others are more of a "unless there's a significant community issue with this, we will go ahead" proposition, which is how we bring new elders to the community. Some personnel issues also fit this category (such as new hires).

Elder decisions tend to be high-level directional issues regarding doctrine or personnel. Decisions regarding our doctrinal statements, church discipline with community members or letting a staff member go are handled exclusively at the elder level.

Our first step is often an attempt to discern which category a particular situation or decision falls under. As with all things, we try to do this through prayer, discussion and consensus as leaders.

But surely it's not all that easy, is it? Of course not. Craig Van Gelder highlights some of the issues of communal discernment in a postmodern context:

> Diverse perspectives, rooted in different methods and the particulars of social location, bring a multi-perspectival dynamic into any discussion. Rather than playing out these differences around power dynamics related to personalities, roles, or the vote of the majority, which is so often the case in congregations, a more redemptive approach is to engage such differences through a process of mutual discernment. This requires leadership. This requires time. This requires a mutual commitment among those who are around the table. And this requires being Spirit-led. Reflected in this approach is the important theoretical insight that we need to develop a practice of "communicative reason" within diverse communities in order to come to shared conclusions.[4]

This "multi-perspectival dynamic" he mentions will be especially true in newer, mission-driven churches, which tend to attract people from a broad range of churched and nonchurched backgrounds. The challenge is leading a group of Christians who have been hurt and are especially sensitive to and suspicious of leadership and people who are not yet sure where they stand on the person of Jesus or the institution of the church. It is especially challenging to lead them into healthy forward motion on vital issues facing the community.

Our conviction is this: all three of these kinds of decisions need to be present regularly in a healthy missional community. If you look at your way of moving forward as a church and find that all your decisions tend to be any one of these categories (for example, all decisions are made by congregational vote or all decisions are made by elder pronouncement), something is out of balance and needs to be adjusted. Even a community in which all decisions are made by elder recommendations or proposals is not ideal. At times leaders have to make hard calls, and at other times they must allow the community to wrestle through tough decisions and formulate possible solutions. A healthy and mature community will do each of these in balance. Further, we have found amazing trust built in our communities when the elders give up making all the decisions on their own and either submit some of their recommendations to the community for affirmation or simply ask the community to come to consensus on an issue and advise the elders of their thinking.

PRACTICALLY SPEAKING

In practice, our seasons of discernment have ranged from three months to a year, focused on a particular question or topic. They often start and end with prayer meetings. As a community, we have generally eschewed anything like a business meeting but have always incorporated prayer, silence and reflection, and listening into our times of discernment. In that way, we draw from the Quaker tradition, in that we desire these times to be meetings for worship in which business is conducted and direction discerned.[5]

Bookended by these times of prayer are online and in-person discussions, both formal and informal. We use these discussions to attempt to answer questions and objections and to make sure that all viewpoints are heard. We have one elder in particular who is skilled in getting us to the place where everyone feels that they have been heard and understood, whether we go in their desired direction or not. We can't overstate how important this is in building trust between the community and its leaders.

The less formal conversations generally take place in home groups, around tables or among other small groups or between individuals. We use these meetings to get a sense of where the community is at as we seek consensus and the answer to the question "What are we hearing from God?"

At the end of one of these seasons, we often reach that place where we can say, "It seems good to the Holy Spirit and to us," and we are able to move ahead. In cases where that is not true, we generally forgo moving ahead in favor of further discussion and prayer. And when further discussion and prayer fail to yield consensus, we often take that as a sign from God that now is not the time. Often we have seen God bring tabled topics back up in our community, such as our Sunday-morning space, when the community was not ready to make a move, but later was.

When it seems the community is showing reticence and yet the elders feel it mission-critical to make a decision, we have seen our role as heating up the conversation and keeping the important questions out there until we sense the community more willing to engage them.

ALLOWING THE PROCESS TO WORK

We recognize that this is hard, slow work, especially if your context tends to be congregational, has strong elder rule or looks to paid staff for all major decisions. But as we said earlier, we are convinced that our job as leaders is not to make all the decisions or to abdicate that responsibility to majority rule. It is to lead the community through times of discernment with a view toward the whole community maturing together toward Christlikeness and, in the process, joining God's mission. That maturity process is too often short-circuited in congregational settings by the loudest voices or the biggest contributors and in top-heavy elder- or staff-ruled settings where leaders make decisions and give pronouncements with no view to allowing the community entrée into the process and thus into the growth that the process provides.

You may think that sounds like a long, time-consuming

process. It is. But again, our job is not simply to lead or to do all the ministry ourselves. Our job is to equip the people for the work of ministry (Ephesians 4:11-13). That means allowing them to participate in the stretching, growth-inducing work of prayer and discernment in many things big and small.

Yes, as we've said, there are times when elders need to make decisions that are not really proper for public discussion (as when letting a staff member go or when making salary decisions). But more often than not, our role is giving attention to an issue ("Has anyone else noticed this is a problem [or need]?") and inviting the community into helping discern solutions ("What do you hear God saying as you pray about what we ought to do?").

DECISION MAKING IN THE ELDER SETTING

Practically speaking, this means that we rarely (if ever) take votes as an elder team. Rather, we pray, we listen to God and each other, and we try to find areas of agreement and consensus. In times when consensus is not to be found, we allow the process to continue, trusting that God is at work even in our disagreements. That is, we find that God is able to form us through healthy conflict much more than through quick agreement.

But what about when nearly the whole team is in favor of moving one way, and one person dissents? Often we do our best to listen and hear the reason behind the dissent, even going so far as to reflect back what we have heard and asking that elder, "Are we hearing you correctly? Is there anything you are trying to say that we have missed?" When this is done well, our experience is that the dissenting person, secure in the knowledge that he or she has been heard, is almost always willing to lay down his or her right to hold up the process and to support the general consensus.

This is often a much longer process than just taking a vote and moving on. But in the congregational process, we have rarely looked back and felt that we took too long to make a decision. If anything, it's been the opposite: we've felt as though we didn't give enough time to process and so short-circuited something that perhaps God wanted to do or that we later saw to be a better direction or decision.

But What If We Made the Wrong Decision?

So, if we do all of these things in the right order and measure, God will always guide us to the right decision, correct? Well, that depends on what you mean by "right."

At times we as a community and we as an elder team have prayerfully worked through a discernment process, felt we had the consensus not just on the direction but also on the means of stepping out in faith . . . only to have the whole thing come crashing down around us.

Did we do it wrong? Were we deceived? Did we only *think* we heard from God?

We have come to see that growth as a community and as leaders is facilitated more by failures than by successes. By *growth*, we do not mean the numbers of people attending your church or your reputation as a leader. We are talking about the maturity of your community and the wisdom you carry as a leader. God has given us many opportunities to experience grace in community as a reality and not just as a theological construct by failing—and forgiving—together.

And when I look back on "wrong" decisions through that lens, I'm truly able to thank God, not only for the decisions that turned out well, but also for the ones that didn't—and for the formation and learning that took place through truly owning the ones that didn't. In fact, the lessons learned through the decisions that went sideways are more deeply embedded in our hearts and are more valuable to us as elders than many of our "right" decisions, which generally are pretty quickly forgotten.

God leads us as a church and as leaders, but he never promises us an unblemished record of successes. What he does promise is to bring redemption and beauty out of our failures. And for that, we can give thanks.

10

The Difficult Tasks of Elders

*Tell Archippus: "See to it that you complete
the work you have received in the Lord."*

PAUL, TO THE CHURCH IN COLOSSAE

*We work in the confidence that God is
able to give us the gifts and graces needed
for ministry in our time and place.*

WILL WILLIMON, PASTOR

The work of eldership is at times both difficult and joyous—hard work and fun play. And when people come together around the person of Jesus and the mission of church, united in heart and soul for the good of their community and congregation, even the hard work can be fun. But that doesn't change the fact that there are difficult, soul-straining tasks to be tackled. Budgets, annual reports, decision making—these are one kind of difficult. But at a much deeper level is the soul work that elders do in their communities—the spiritual tilling, planting and sowing, weeding and harvesting that constitutes the true work of church leadership.

Few of us understand the scope of responsibility when we are invited into eldership, but we soon discover that it can be overwhelming. Better men and women than you or I have struggled mightily with the weight of responsibility of church leadership. This is especially true in mission communities that place a high value on not only caring for those in the community, but also carefully and intentionally reaching beyond their church walls in love and service. When a church is truly effective in mission, it faces questions and challenges above and beyond what many church communities face.

In Colossians, Paul includes a little personal note to Archippus: "See to it that you complete the work you have received in the Lord" (Colossians 4:17). Archippus was apparently the one who was left as the pastor when Epaphras, who planted the church in Colossae, left to be with Paul. And so Paul, ever the encourager, gives him that little pastoral pick-me-up. As spiritual leaders, that's something we need to hear often.

It's with that in mind and with an aim of helping you navigate the tossing seas of eldership and ministry that we look at the difficult tasks of an elder. Be encouraged; it's hard, but God is with us.

PROTECTION

One of the chief metaphors used in Scripture for eldership is that of shepherding. "So guard yourselves and God's people. Feed and shepherd God's flock—his church, purchased with his own blood—over which the Holy Spirit has appointed you as elders" (Acts 20:28 NLT).

This task of guarding our flocks and ourselves is one of the most important given to elders, and yet it is often one of the most overlooked. Too often leadership teams get bogged down in the politics, administration and organization of a church and completely miss the spiritual realities of what is happening both in their own souls and around them; they don't always see how their health as individuals and as a team contributes to the health of their community and how unhealthy individuals or influences can wreak havoc in a church.

My (Bob's) community has been blessed with both a surplus of truly healthy people and a lack of disturbed individuals out to do damage. That doesn't mean, however, that we haven't had any. Every church will at one point or another have to deal with hurt people who intentionally hurt people or those who seem bent on doing damage to a community.

I recall one person in particular that came to our community under the guise of great interest in what we were doing, a desire to be taught and to teach others. Fortunately, we tend to take things slow with people, because after a short season, he began picking verbal fights with leaders and other members of the community, criticizing our liturgy because we weren't doing it "right," and even going so far as to call some members of the community heretical. After he left, he started blogging incessantly about our church and about me in particular. Especially worrisome were some of the veiled threats in his blog posts; I started paying better attention to whether or not my doors were locked at night. I think I may be the only pastor in history to be called both a left-wing heretic and a raging right-wing fundamentalist by the same critic. I'm breathing a bit easier now that he's left town. He has not only left Portland, but Christianity as well.

During the first year of our church's formation, I had an interesting dream: My wife and I were sitting in the living room of a couple that was new to our church. As we talked, I began to get a sense that something was wrong. At a certain point, the couple pulled off the masks they had been wearing and revealed demonic faces. I woke up in a sweat, wondering, *What was that about?*

Shortly after this, a new couple began coming around our Sunday gatherings. On paper, they were exactly what our young community needed: stable, middle-aged folks whose kids had already grown and who had a history of church involvement. At first, I had great hopes that they would be the kinds of mentors we needed. But pretty quickly I began to get a strange vibe from them. It was never something I could pinpoint exactly.

My wife and I were invited to dinner at their place, and in dinner conversation we began to discern that this couple was not only relationally unhealthy, but also involved in some fairly esoteric types of non-Christian spirituality. After that, I paid close attention to them and to who they were connecting with in our community, thinking that maybe my dream had meant something after all. They disappeared not long after, and though I can't be sure, I sensed that my dream was God's way of telling me to keep my eyes open for those who may at first seem like just the kind of people we needed in our new church, but who would turn out to be anything but.

Paul cautions the Ephesian elders to guard themselves and God's people, and then says, "I know that false teachers, like vicious wolves, will come in among you after I leave, not sparing the flock" (Acts 20:29 NLT). Jesus himself warned that we should "beware of false prophets who come disguised as harmless sheep but are really vicious wolves" (Matthew 7:15 NLT). While these warnings speak directly to false teachers and prophets, we shouldn't assume that they are the only kinds of wolves we will encounter when leading our communities. There are those who bring false teaching. There are those who are out to relationally—or even sexually—exploit others.[1] There are those who seem to thrive on causing relational dissension and divisions.

Finding the right balance in dealing with such folks is a constant challenge. But if we are to guard the flock entrusted to us, as Paul instructed the Ephesian elders, we must approach potentially dysfunctional personalities carefully and with prayer. Jesus himself cautioned his disciples to be as innocent as doves and yet as shrewd as snakes (Matthew 10:16). We don't need to be stirring up trouble in our communities just because we don't like or agree with someone, but neither should we be naïve as to the kinds of damage some folks could inflict on our church.

This is truly a whole elder team job. Don't leave it to the lead pastor to identify and deal with these folks. Approach it as a whole team, making note in your meetings of those who might be troubled, those who might be hurt (and in need of care) and those who might be hurting others (in need of a firmer hand).

Recognize wolves for what they are, and deal with them quickly. A failure to address them could damage or derail mission in your church. Simply looking the other way or sweeping it under the rug is not faithful leadership. So make sure you are talking "people stuff" in your leadership meetings and learn to listen to the hunches of the people on your team when they tell you they have an uncomfortable feeling about someone.

Pray through the list of people in your community regularly, listening to what God is saying to you about them. And when and if you do need to confront someone to protect others, do yourselves a favor and have two elders talk to that person. While it's best (and biblical) to confront sin one-on-one first (Matthew 18:15), when you are dealing with people you suspect might be hurting others—not with the kind of rough edges we all have, but by being intentionally divisive, predatory or otherwise a danger to your community—it's always best to have a couple of witnesses.

Also write down your reflections and recollections after the meeting. Share them with the other elders as soon as possible.

It's amazing all the trouble one person can stir up in a community when she sets her mind to distort the truth of what has been said to her or how she has been treated. The truth plus or minus 10 percent can be just as damaging as blatant lies.

On the other hand, don't make the opposite mistake and label anyone who disagrees with you or your agenda as a wolf. A safe community is one in which people do not march in lockstep, in the faux unity of doing or agreeing with whatever their leaders do or say, but have the freedom to ask questions, have the space to give respectful pushback and understand their role in stewarding the vision and mission of the church. There's a huge difference between someone who is hurting and struggling with church, perhaps projecting their issues with leaders onto you, and someone who is truly unteachable and beyond listening to pastoral exhortations and so must be dealt with in the firmest of manners.

Be sure to check your heart before allowing yourself to put someone in the category of "wolf." Ask yourself, "What does this person bring up in me, and why?" and "Why might he be acting the way he is? Is there some underlying issue that could be addressed pastorally?" If you have done that prayerfully and are sure that what's happening is not your garden-variety authority issues or the result of you projecting your own issues onto them, it's time to deal with them.

I (Bob) am a firm believer in getting people to self-select out of a community, as opposed to kicking them out. The way I have seen this work time and again is simple: Say the thing that will get them to leave. Think carefully about what they are looking to do or become in your community, and let them know it's not going to happen. It may be as simple as "I really don't feel like we're going to be comfortable trusting you with leadership in our community." Or "we have talked and prayed through this doctrinal [or practical or ecclesiological] issue as a leadership team, and I can't see that we're going to change any time soon." Generally, once people know that you know what they are up to because you have drawn a line in the sand, keeping them from getting what they want, they tend to move on.

Protection from disunity. On Jesus' heart and mind just before his crucifixion was the unity of his followers—that they be together in mission and fellowship (John 17:23). When we get to the Pastoral Epistles, we find this theme emphasized repeatedly. Paul instructs Titus, "If people are causing divisions among you, give a first and second warning. After that, have nothing more to do with them" (Titus 3:10).

There's a kind of personality that naturally causes divisions, and it must be responded to pastorally. These people aren't necessarily wolves. They may be acting out of concern for the community and a perceived problem, but they handle their concern in an immature way, unaware of the impact of their conversations. Or their ideas may be doctrinally or missionally incompatibile with your community. Disunity often happens when people misunderstand something. They either misunderstand your intent as leaders in going in a certain direction or making a particular decision, or something hard happens and there's a misunderstanding as to what has really happened and what the role of the church leadership has been.

Over the years, we have found ourselves cautioning people on matters doctrinal, personal and relational—all with a view toward the unity of the church. Without unity there is little hope for pursuing God's mission. It sometimes gets back to our pastors or elders that someone told someone else a version of events—say, with someone leaving the community or an interpersonal blowup—that is significantly different from reality. Sometimes we hear the stories and wonder how they got from what actually happened to there; they are so far removed from reality and what they said reflects so poorly on our leadership that we have to wonder if we're even talking about the same event. When this happens, we try to talk to those who are spreading the stories and set them straight. Additionally, we ask them to go to those they have talked to and set them straight as well. Few things have the potential to hurt a church's unity more than people believing the leaders have acted in bad faith, so we take this seriously.

As a missional community, we make room for people at a wide spectrum of places spiritually. That means we always have some people who are a few standard deviations removed from the doctrinal norms of our community. More than once we've had to ask people not to make an issue in the community of their particular doctrinal or spiritual preferences, though we welcome their participation. And if they can't do that, if it's that important to them, we invite them to realize that there may be an incompatibility between them and our community.

We once had a young couple leave our church over the issue of head coverings. Though they could see this was not our practice when they first started attending our community, it was important enough to them that they left when I let them know we would never ask the women of our church to cover their heads.

I was sorry to see them go; they were truly a nice young couple with a lot of potential for leadership and ministry to others in our community. But there was a fundamental disconnect between how they saw women in the church and how we did. They thought women ought to cover their heads in worship, and we saw that as a culturally bound command. I was sorry to see them go but glad they chose not to make an issue of head coverings.

When you see people talking or acting in a way that has the potential to or is already causing some disunity in the community, warn them. And by "warn them" I don't think Paul means "Stop it or else!" I think he means to appeal to their sense of community. Warn them about how what they are doing or saying has the potential to hurt or even destroy the community. Appeal to their conscience. Perhaps the second warning might need to be stern, but we'd suggest starting with a more pastoral approach. And if all your warnings go unheeded, if they refuse to listen and truly cause damage to your church, suggest that they need to look elsewhere for a community that will be more in line with what they desire in a church.

CORRECTION

Elders are to be the teachers of the church. Not just the senior or teaching pastor, but each individual and the team as a whole ought to have the kind of gentle, humble and wise presence that leads others to listen and to move to align their lives with the character of Christ and the purposes of God in the world. As we wrote earlier, one of the requirements of elders is that they be "able to teach" and "able to encourage others with wholesome teaching and show those who oppose it where they are wrong" (1 Timothy 3:2; Titus 1:9 NLT).

Generally, the kinds of correcting that elders need to do are the kinds that Priscilla and Aquila did with Apollos (Acts 18:26): they explained to him more accurately the way of the Lord. He knew a lot and had great enthusiasm, and yet a couple of his doctrinal points were a little off. He didn't yet know about Christian baptism and probably a few other things. So they came alongside and helped him to understand. This is a great picture of what elders do. They encourage others in the knowledge of Jesus and in following in his way. Don't be afraid to teach others what you have learned about following Jesus, especially those under your elder or pastoral care.

However, it's good to know what the essentials are as well as what doctrinal differences your community is okay with. This is something you should talk about early on with your elder team:

what is our doctrinal statement, and how closely do we want people to adhere to it in order to become a part of our community? Once you've done that and defined your essentials, don't feel like you need to correct others outside that scope. We have a biblical mandate to go to the mat over two main things: "Who is Jesus?" and "What is the gospel?" (see Galatians 1:8). I (Bob) find most of the correcting I do leading back to those two questions: whether someone has (1) too legalistic or too libertine views of the Christian life (a solid knowledge of the gospel corrects both) or (2) a false understanding of who God is and what he wants from us (knowing and understanding the person of Jesus roots us in this). All things major seem to come back to those two things. With most everything else, I make room for discussion, giving my opinion, but I don't worry overmuch whether others see it my way.

In regard to the Christian life, I do my best to root ethics and morals in the person of Jesus and in the New Testament ethics the apostles gave us. The correcting I do is pastoral, with a view toward helping someone understand that her views or actions don't fit into the character of Christ. We want to correct poor moral behavior when we see it, but we resist becoming moralistic in our gospel. The good news of Jesus isn't simply that he has shown us the right way to live; it's that he's lived it for us, on our behalf. And our righteousness is rooted in his character and life, not in our own. Our own righteousness comes as grateful obedience because we have believed the good news of what Jesus has done for us.

As elders, we want people to live Christlike lives, but we do our best to see that happen through our preaching of the gospel; we do not act as the doctrine or morals police. However, there will be times when we need to move from an encouraging or correcting stance to a disciplinary one. We'll talk about that later.

Correction of poor teaching. Some people have views that diverge from the mainstream of your community and tradition, but do not quite rise to the level of "false teachers." They are in positions of influence in your community, but they are pushing doctrines or influences that are out of step with where the leadership feels the community needs to be or go.

Often people bring the doctrinal and practical baggage of their upbringing into our communities and need the time and space to work through that. But occasionally a home community leader or theology discussion leader wants to push things in a direction you are not comfortable with. In these cases, it's best to talk face to face. Email and social media exchanges have a way of turning negative way too quickly because they do not involve facial expressions, body language or tone of voice. People tend to read the harshest possible tone into them. When you feel the need to bring someone closer to the vision and mission of your community, do a couple of things.

First, do your best to understand where they are coming from. There's a reason they are bringing this emphasis, and maybe it's not just a pet doctrine of theirs. Maybe there is an imbalance that needs to be corrected in your community. Maybe there's an area that has been corporately neglected and together you can find a way to address that.

Second, if they are convinced that this teaching is beneficial for the community, and you remain skeptical, but if it is not a major doctrinal or moral issue, ask them to teach comparatively, giving more than one perspective. It's fine if they say, "This is my perspective," as long as they commit to presenting a fair and balanced reading of other perspectives on the issue as well. Also, at times, after giving my view, I have mentioned that "such and such a leader in our community sees it this way." Far from being confusing, this tends to help people to feel safe, to feel that they are being given the whole story, theologically speaking. This drives people to think and read and pray through issues on their own.

Third, if you feel a particular emphasis just isn't helpful, and it's becoming unhealthy for your community, urge the person to press pause, to take some time to discuss with the elders why it is so important to them and to be open to hearing other sides.

When all has been said and done, if someone feels that her particular eschatological position or charismatic inclination is so important to her that she is unwilling to soften it or let it go, and yet it is out of step with your leadership and community, it might be best to recommend to her some communities that might be a better fit for her.

Correcting other leaders. One of the hardest tasks you will face in leadership is correcting another leader. Our fears and insecurities—over confronting someone else or over being confronted—can make this uncomfortable in the extreme. However, if you have built a team that values relationships, that listens to and loves one another, this will be not only easier but also necessary at some points.

All of us have growth areas, and it's up to the elders of the church to help each other grow.

When it becomes clear that an elder is moving off track, though not yet in a way that would disqualify him, it's best to have someone on your team talk to him friend to friend, give feedback on what he or she sees happening, inquire as to what's happening, explore what the state of his heart and mind might be, and ask how they can help.

Should it become more serious, remember the relationship first and foremost. If you have to use authority (saying to a pastor, "I'm an elder and that makes me your boss"), that may win a particular battle, but the war will be lost. Here's a bit of wisdom a pastoral mentor of mine gave me: When having to confront a staff member or elder, it's best if that confrontation can come from someone above or beside her in the organizational structure of a community. Asking a staff elder (an elder who is paid) to confront someone they technically report to can damage or hinder their working relationship. Protect it by tasking someone else with working through the issues.

One verse that often comes up in this discussion is "do not entertain an accusation against an elder unless it is brought by two or three witnesses" (1 Timothy 5:19). This should be read as a guideline, not something to be followed legalistically. Even if you have only one person accusing an elder of something serious, like child abuse or adultery, take it seriously. Attempt to discover the truth. Even if no one can attest to the sin in question, it may be enough to hear from that elder's spouse that he or she has suspected something or that there have been significant difficulties in the marriage. Don't rush to judgment, but don't sit on the sidelines either, waiting for more people to come forward with accusations—especially with serious charges. However, when someone claims an elder has, say, a significant issue with anger, and you and the other elders have experienced that person as gracious, patient and loving, take the accusation with a grain of salt. That's the kind of thing two or three others need to confirm.

Should an elder need to be asked to step down, make as much of it public as possible. Paul continues: "Those who sin should be reprimanded in front of the whole church; this will serve as a strong warning to others" (1 Timothy 5:20 NLT). This doesn't mean a public dressing down in front of the whole community, but while respecting the privacy of the elder being asked to step down as much as possible, the basics of the story and your response as leaders should be shared with the community. This prevents a situation arising where information leaks out a little at a time. Share your love and concern for the people involved, let the community know you have had to make a hard decision and tell them *as much as possible*. Also, we have found it helpful to make announcements like this in person to the whole community before doing so in writing or online.

Church Discipline

As hard as correcting another leader is, an even more difficult task an elder team will face is church discipline. When someone has been spoken to and has been warned of the damaging effects of their behavior, and yet persists in sin, your leadership team has no choice but to move to a stance of church discipline. Generally this involves escalating from having one or two elders speak to someone to inviting the accused to speak to the whole leadership team together. We have found that most people opt out at this point.

It's not that our elder team is scary, but actually having to defend a behavior in a context other than a personal conversation is often too much. Tragically, they choose to withdraw from the community. There will be times, however, when they want to continue to consider themselves members of the community, even though they are disregarding what the leaders and the majority of the community have to say.

Generally, most church discipline cases I have seen involve sexual issues. It seems that the choices people make in regard to their sexuality have a sacrosanct status in our culture. To call someone out on his or her sexual sin is seen as so intrusive that it's a greater offense than the sin being confronted. Wives leaving husbands, husbands cheating on their wives, overly domineering and abusive spouses—you will likely face all of these as a community.

An often misquoted verse in Scripture is "do not judge, or you too will be judged" (Matthew 7:1). You can almost count on hearing it sometime in a process of church discipline, either from the person being confronted or from someone defending him or her. Less often quoted is Paul's admonition to church leaders, "It isn't my responsibility to judge outsiders, but it certainly is your responsibility to judge those inside the church who are sinning" (1 Corinthians 5:12 NLT).

Of course, we always attempt to confront sin privately. When it becomes apparent that something has reached an "elder level" of needing to be dealt with, we generally ask, "Who has the strongest relational ties with the person? To whom is he most likely to listen?" We send that person and one other to have a conversation with the person privately (or sometimes a series of conversations). We hope and pray for repentance, a change of heart and mind about the matter. We ask those elders to continue to check in with him and to provide the challenge and the support necessary to make changes.

When there isn't repentance, we ask the person to come and talk over the matter with the whole elder team. As mentioned earlier, many opt out. We do our best to pursue further communication and relationship with that person, but usually all we can do beyond continued pleas for repentance is to offer whatever help we can to those who have been and are being impacted by his decisions.

Should it come to a place where the person neither wishes to repent nor wishes to withdraw from the community, we make the hard decision: we ask him to leave, always with an invitation to continue the dialogue and return to the community should repentance and resolution occur. This must be handled carefully, with prayer and much communication between the elder team and the community.

Rarely does it get to the point where you will need to stand before the whole church and, in line with 1 Corinthians 5:4-5 and Matthew 18:17, tell them of your communication with the unrepentant person, his or her unwillingness to listen and to see change happen, and the elder team's desire that he withdraw from full or even minimal participation in the community. In fact, we pray it never gets to that place for you. But if it does, make sure that the community knows not just the facts but also your hearts: how you have come to the conclusion as a team that the behavior is sinful, the persistent unrepentance you encountered and your corporate desire as elders to see something redemptive happen. Emphasize your love not just for the unrepentant person, but also for the community as whole. And then let them know that you have asked the person to withdraw from the community in the hopes that losing community will wake him up to the realities of what is happening in his life.

What should the orientation of the community toward that person be from there? We don't suggest shunning them—that is, refusing to speak to him or unfriending him, but rather that the community would listen to the words of Jesus and treat him as a pagan or a tax collector. And how did Jesus treat those people? With love, but clearly recognizing that they were not in a place of repentance, not able to be entrusted with leadership in the community, not to be included in the decision-making processes of the community—but also not to be treated as a pariah.[2]

Practically, this means revoking his "membership" or "covenant participant" status in your church. Love him, but love him as you would the non-Christian his is behaving like. Paul encourages us to "hand [them] over to Satan" (1 Corinthians 5:5), which means that we abandon them to the consequences of their actions, even as we pray that those consequences will bring about a godly repentance.

Paul also says we should throw them out (1 Corinthians 5:2, 13). I believe in context this refers to blatant, unrepentant sin of an egregious public nature, like sleeping with their stepmother or leaving their spouse and bringing their new lover to church with them (as I've seen happen a number of times). At this point, they are so far beyond the pale that even the invitation to attendance at your public gatherings should be withdrawn. In the case of really damaging, unrepentant, public sin, you may need to caution your people to dial down their friendships with that person—not to the point of elimination (because we want to leave room for redemptive conversations to happen) but certainly to say, "I can't pretend this isn't happening. I don't want to lose our friendship, but until we deal with this in a God-honoring way, it can't be like it was before."

Protecting Other Communities

It's not uncommon to hear through the grapevine that a person who has left your community in an unrepentant state or because she was called out on her divisiveness will find her way to another church community. Don't let that community learn the hard way what you have learned about the damage this person can inflict. Don't let the person under church discipline just sneak off to another church community. Task someone on your team with contacting the elders of her new church and communicating the story of your experience with her. Leaders in the other church may or may not be receptive to hearing this, but you owe them at least the courtesy of trying.

Firing Staff or Disqualifying Elders

Probably the hardest of all elder tasks is letting go of a staff member or asking an elder to step down. These circumstances rarely involve issues that rise to a church discipline level, but rather happen because a staff member is underperforming, or there has been a relational breakdown that seems irreparable, or an elder is managing his family or home poorly (1 Timothy 3:4-5). Of course, letting someone go or even asking her to step down from a leadership position should never be taken lightly, done quickly or done without much prayer and discussion by the whole elder team (minus, of course, the person being discussed). Reconciliation involves giving the person a chance, giving invitations to change and waiting to see those changes take hold.

However, sometimes the whole elder team recognizes that the situation has become unworkable. In those cases, the tough call must be made, and the team should be in agreement. Be careful of moving on something like this without consensus or at least with the assurance that anyone on your elder team who disagrees with the conclusion understands the position of the rest of the team and will support the decision publicly.

Most mistakes we have seen (or made) in this regard have centered on moving too quickly, not allowing enough time for change or not communicating enough with the community what can be communicated within the bounds of confidentiality. It's hard to move too slowly with such a decision, but it's easy to move too quickly. Make sure your process includes a lot of time for prayer and discernment by all involved, as much love and care as possible, and as much listening to the person being let go as you can bear.

Here are a few considerations for letting a staff member go. First, be as generous as you can. If you can provide severance, do it. Be sacrificial, in fact. Though their employment in your community is coming to an end, your responsibility to their family remains. Do whatever you can to help them land on their feet.

Second, to the extent that you can, protect the relationships and reputation of the staff member you have to let go. You may know "the whole story," but the community doesn't have to. Yes, this means that some will never understand the way they would if you laid out all the shortcomings and relational errors that led to the person being let go, but that's part of the cost you will bear on their behalf.

Third, in terms of either a staff member or an elder, when it has become clear that they are no longer effective in their position of leadership, do what you can to help them come to that conclusion on their own. Pastors and elders have lives and growth curves, and when their family dynamics or personal struggles make it clear to the rest of the team that they need a break, do your best to help them come to that realization. It may mean asking some good, probing questions like "How has what's been happening in your family been impacting your ability to care for others in our community?" or "What would you say your passion for this position is over and against what it was when you started?" Mutually agreed upon sabbaticals are great for staff or elders in helping them gain some perspective and work through the issues that the elder team would like to see addressed. If you can give that to them, do it. Check in toward the end of the time to see what progress has been made before any final decisions are made.

The old adage "hindsight is 20/20" will never feel as apropos as in the letting go of a staff member. You can do everything you know to do, approach the situation with as much care and concern as you can muster, and it can *still* go sideways on you. Know that even in your mistakes, even in your mishandled situations, God is still present, still leading your team in learning. Own any mistakes made in the process, confess when necessary and continue to do your best to move forward in love and mission.

HEALING

One of the greatest privileges we have as elders is participating in healing. We join with God in the mission of bringing redemption and healing to the world through service and spreading the good news of what Jesus has done in our cities and towns. We see good news come alive in the healing of our communities. And though it's a privilege to be a part of God's healing work, that doesn't mean it's not a difficult task.

Healing the community. Occasionally, traumatic events happen to communities as a whole: someone dies tragically, a much-loved staff member is let go, a pastor washes out of ministry for moral reasons. All of these require an elder team to ask not just "How can we handle this?" but "How can we help healing happen in our community?"

Take the long view. Your community needs healing, but healing is a process. Often, only time and an elder team with a listening, attentive stance toward the community will bring the kind of redemptive outcome you would like to see from these hard situations. You might find yourself saying, "I wish they could all get over this!" They wish they could too, but unless you let the process of grieving work itself out, unless you let God do his healing work in your community (and this is something God seems to take a decent amount of time to do), you'll end up compounding the hurt.

When a terrible situation arises, offer the ears of the elder team. When it's the elder team as a whole that has contributed to the hurt (such as in a firing), offer more than ears, offer presence, whether at town hall meetings for your community, in home groups or one-on-one. In that way they can listen and give perspective in a nondefensive way.

Pray for the growth of your community through hard circumstances. Avoid blaming the difficult things on God, but strenuously point to the growth that can happen when difficult things are handled well. All in all, recognize that you as an elder team are responsible not just to make difficult decisions, but also to care for those affected by them.

Healing for individuals. James 5:14 makes it clear: the elders have a responsibility to pray for the healing of individuals within their community. "Is any one of you sick? He should call the elders of the church to pray over him and anoint him with oil in the name of the Lord." Whether or not you are part of a tradition that considers itself charismatic, healing prayer ought to be a part of your elder ministry. Even in noncharismatic churches, it can and should be done carefully and with faith in the God we are asking to bring healing.

I (Bob) like to take a formational approach to this ministry. While not suggesting that God has brought illness into someone's life for a particular reason,[3] I want to gently push them toward an awareness of what God has been doing and could do through their experience of being sick. Healing then, as James points out, becomes not just a physical but a spiritual, soul and heart issue as well. It also becomes a chance to point to God's presence in the life of someone who may be tempted by her illness to believe that God has abandoned her. To this end I usually bring along a small bottle of a fragrant essential oil and anoint the person as we pray, explaining that in Scripture, anointing with oil is a sign of the presence of the Holy Spirit. In this way we declare the presence of God even in the midst of the person's pain.

A young man in our community was suffering from a severe problem with one of his eyes. Pressure was building up and threatening to take his sight. Josh underwent an operation on that eye, and for a season all was well, until the problem resurfaced. At that point he invited the elders of our community to gather with him for prayer. In talking with him before we prayed, I asked, "What has been going on inside you because of this?" He told us that the recurrence of the problem, and the pain that went along with it, not to mention the hindrance to his work, had brought up a lot of issues of anger, of pride and of self-reliance that he knew he needed to work on.

After talking about this a bit, I asked him my final question: "Hypothetically, if you had to choose between God healing your eye or God healing your anger and pride, which would you choose?" He thought for a moment and then quietly responded, "My anger and pride." We prayed for Josh, his eye was healed, and he has since made great progress in dealing with his anger and other issues. At other times, we have asked those questions, and while not seeing physical healing, we have helped people to at least connect with what God was forming in them through their illness.

When praying for those in our community, we do so with faith, knowing that God loves the people for whom we are praying and wants to see them made like Christ, and that whether or not he chooses to physically heal them right then, he will heal them someday in the resurrection. In that faith, we humbly ask God to bring not only physical but also spiritual healing to redeem their suffering through growth and not let it be wasted. We never "declare" someone healed, but we always hold out hope that they will be. We believe that "praying in faith" means not that we will see things turn out exactly as we would want to see them, but grasping tightly to faith in the One to whom we pray, to his loving care and providential presence in our lives.

In all of these difficult tasks and the many we haven't covered here, know that God is with you in the starting of your community, in the nurturing of it and in the day-to-day ups and downs of ministry. This is easy to believe in the ups, but it's essential to believe in the downs.

11

What About Women Elders?

Women and men are indeed very different, and those differences are essential to how God empowers each to induce the Kingdom of God into their specific life setting and ministry. What we lose by excluding the distinctively feminine from "official" ministries of teaching and preaching is of incalculable value. That loss is one of a few fundamental factors which account for the astonishing weakness of "the Church" in the contemporary context.

DALLAS WILLARD, FOREWORD TO *HOW I CHANGED MY MIND ABOUT WOMEN IN LEADERSHIP*

In my own experience, I cannot deny God's mighty work in and through the lives of gifted women teachers—women who have taught me a great deal about the Scriptures and what a life with God looks like. They have helped me pursue the heart of the Father and His mission more faithfully. What am I to do with that?

SCOT MCKNIGHT, *JUNIA IS NOT ALONE*

Whether women should be considered leaders, pastors and elders is a subject of significant debate and, at times, contention, in the church today. For some denominations, the issue of women in leadership is strongly rejected, while it is widely accepted in other denominations. At times it might be tempting to believe that those who are on the other side of the issue than you don't hold Scripture highly or believe in its truth. Wisdom shows us that this thinking is to be avoided. It is important, however, to wrestle with this issue, as it has significant implications on the pursuit of God's mission in community. It is also crucial that we realize there are those who love God, love people and love the Word of God on both sides of this issue.

We've written this book from the standpoint of affirming women in every area of church leadership. Though not at the level of "what is the gospel?" and "who is Jesus?" it remains for us an important issue because of who we believe Jesus to be and what the gospel is. We recognize that you may not share this conviction with us. In light of that, we desire to write in a way that is helpful for both complementarian and egalitarian churches. Our desire is to see strong communities moving out on mission, led by faithful, qualified elders committed to the gospel of Jesus. Period.

However, we believe that it is essential to understand the New Testament texts on women in light of first-century culture. We must also take into account the desire of the New Testament writers to have the gospel seen as attractive and yet challenging to culture, and not destabilizing to first-century households. Without these understandings, we could easily land at a place of raising what was necessary *then* to something mandatory *now* and of making a universal (no women in leadership) out of something that biblically wasn't universal.

We believe that God's redemptive ethos runs throughout all of human history, spanning from Genesis to Revelation. Read in light of this, we have to ask, "Why were the words of the Bible written? What is the intent behind them?" We see this redemptive spirit permeating all of Scripture, and historically women and their role in ministry expanded as the Bible's plot moved forward; it didn't grow smaller. God's movement of redemption channels its renewing spirit into a modern world with power to change social structure and direction to guide the renewal process.[1]

If Paul did reserve eldership in the church to men only, we believe he did so primarily because women in leadership would be a stumbling block to the gospel message in that particular culture and context. Remember, Paul is a missiologist, always thinking through how the message of the gospel is most accurately and effectively communicated to those who need to hear of the life, death and resurrection of Jesus. Let us not presume that a careful look at the cultural context of New Testament comments regarding women is simply a progressive slide that bows to cultural preferences.

Many complementarians point out Peter's words regarding male headship (1 Peter 3:1-6), claiming that this is a consistent principle for all time. Yet the same passage includes Peter's instruction that women are to refrain from braiding their hair and wearing gold and fine clothing as simply a cultural element for that particular context. They claim the former passage is for all time, but the latter is simply for "just then." Others point out that Ephesians 5 says that wives should submit to their husbands (v. 22) and yet miss the significant directive in the previous verse: "Submit to *one another* out of reverence to Christ" (v. 21, emphasis added). In a spirit of reverence and honor to the risen Lord, we yield to one another—regardless of gender (see also Galatians 3:28; 1 Peter 2:9-10).

Paul writes in 1 Corinthians that women should prophesy with their heads covered (11:5); then three chapters later he says that women are to remain silent (14:34). How can one prophesy when remaining silent? Another example is found in 1 Timothy 2:11-12, which clearly states that no woman should teach or exercise authority over a man. How can one prophesy out loud and yet at the same time learn quietly with all submissiveness? If we simply take Paul's writings on women as universal, then he was blatantly contradicting himself in several places.

We believe the purpose of these passages isn't to address universal principles for the role of women in leadership, but to address cultural understandings of mission and how they impact or hinder the spread of the gospel message. Trying to present that same compelling gospel in our context, while packaging it with a conviction that first-century cultural expectations must apply today, becomes increasingly difficult. In other words, while putting women in places of leadership within local churches was a hindrance to the gospel in the first century, *not* having women in leadership is often a hindrance to the gospel in the twenty-first century.

Numerous books have been written debating egalitarian and complementarian views of Scripture. In the recommended resources at the back of this book, we have listed several that address the topic with greater depth and insight. Our focus in this chapter is not to parse every verb, explore every passage on women in leadership or convince you of our conviction on the issue. Instead, we want to focus on a clear explanation of how participation in God's mission includes the gifts of all people— male and female—in hopes that you will seriously consider the mission-focused perspective of the gospel—maybe from a new angle. While we are unable in this space to deal comprehensively with a topic that whole books have been written about, for those who wonder how we have come to the place of having women in the role of elders, we offer a bit of story, our understanding of Scripture and some caveats.

Our Journey with Women in Leadership

I (Bob) was raised with and even planted our church community with a complementarian view of women in ministry. In all honesty, I was prepared to do whatever I could to get around that. Originally, I envisioned a male elder team for our community that handled the shepherding and a coed leadership team that handled the details of administration and ministry.

But a peculiar thing happened along the way to realizing that structure: I changed. I was challenged to go back to Scripture and to reexamining not only what it said but also what it said against the backdrop of the culture at the time it was said. As a result, I came out at a different place than where I started.

When we planted our church community in 2004, our focus was having a church designed to make sense to and be a home for the unchurched and the formerly churched. I discovered how important the issue of women in leadership was, not only for the people we built our community for but also for those we had built it with. This issue weighed heavily on their minds. Many had come from churches where they had seen women and their contributions to the life of the community marginalized or otherwise downplayed. Those who had little or no church background simply could not wrap their minds around barring someone from leadership because of their gender. In a world where women are the CEOs of companies and the presidents of countries, this position seemed baffling.

When I combined what my community felt and believed with what I was also thinking and feeling, I knew I had to begin a process where we would work through this issue carefully and prayerfully. If we arrived at the complementarian view, fine. At least we would have done our homework and wouldn't ascribe to it because it was "the way we have always done things." If we arrived elsewhere, we knew there would be implications, but we were prepared to deal with them when they arose.

The process started for me (Bob) with a book by William Webb called *Slaves, Women and Homosexuals*. In short, Webb contends that when we compare Scripture against what we know of the cultures in which it was written, it is always progressive in light of those cultures on the issues of slavery and women. That is, Scripture consistently calls the culture to raise the dignity, status and role of women and slaves. Additionally, Scripture is progressive when compared to itself; within the pages of Scripture, there is movement—for example, a progression from what Moses said about women to what Jesus and the New Testament authors said. Webb postulates that within Scripture we can see an ultimate ethic and redemptive arc of freedom and equality, embodied in verses like Galatians 3:28.[2]

We had many long discussions as elders and as a community. As elders we read Sarah Sumner's book *Men and Women in the Church* as well as a few others. We prayed. We talked. We prayed and talked more. At the end of that process of about seven months, we realized we had been led to a different place than where we had started as a community. Following are a few instrumental realizations that got us to where we ended up.

In looking at the way Jesus and the early church dealt with women, we were struck by the fact that Jesus allowed women to follow him. Though not called disciples officially, women were invited to sit in the place of a disciple (Luke 10:38-42).[3] Women were prominent in the early church as deacons (Romans 16:1, in spite of the clear instruction of the apostles in Acts 6 to choose "men") and well known as teachers and coworkers with Paul (for example, Priscilla: Acts 18:26; Romans 16:3). Paul, contrary to much of his culture, advocated that women be taught (1 Timothy 2:11). All of this said to us that God is *still* about raising the status of women.

We also realized that in the New Testament context, women in leadership positions might have been a hindrance for the gospel, particularly among the Jews and in churches with a high percentage of Jewish believers. But in our context, not having women in ministry, or at least not having that role open to them, was an equally large hindrance to the people we were trying to impact.

We looked at all of this and asked ourselves, "Is this an A-level issue?" When we realized it wasn't, we became more comfortable with either outcome. We knew that good Christian churches exist on both sides of the spectrum, and we knew that our commitment to the gospel was strong . . . and so we began to worry less about how others might react to us. If our mission was to reach people, we wanted the offense to be in the gospel, not in our polity, ecclesiastical structure or how we treated half the people who came to our community.

Additionally, we realized that God had specifically placed women in positions of leadership and/or spiritual influence all through Scripture. We noticed numerous examples in the Old Testament. Deborah was the leader of the nation of Israel— whom Scot McKnight called "president, pope and Rambo bundled in one female body."[4] Josiah passed over Jeremiah, Zephaniah, Nahum and Habakkuk when he consulted Huldah, the prophet who singlehandedly brought on Israel's most significant revival.[5] Esther was a queen that God used to save her people, and Miriam was a prophetic national music director.

There were numerous examples in the New Testament we couldn't ignore either: Phoebe was a deacon (that is, a leader in the church) and benefactor of Paul's missions (meaning she probably provided funds and wisdom for Paul on his journeys).[6] Priscilla was a teacher of Apollos, who then taught the church. Romans 16:7 records that Junia was an apostle. However, because of the assumption that women were not allowed to be apostles, Bible translators turned her into a male, naming her Junias. (Junia was a common women's name in the first century while Junias is never documented as a male name.)[7] Romans 16 lists women in leadership positions who worked hard for the Lord—and they weren't just filling communion cups and laying out wafers before the Sunday service. We also read that in the last days sons *and* daughters will prophesy (Acts 2:17).

It was important for us as a community to fully grasp the implications of the resurrection story in John 20. We cannot ignore the fact that the first person commissioned to take the message of Jesus' resurrection to others was Mary Magdalene. A woman is the first person to proclaim to others—to the entire world, for that matter—that Jesus is alive and risen! It seems that in the resurrection there is a radical reevaluation of the role of women in proclamation. It would seem wise then to read 1 Timothy 2 through the lens of passages like Romans 16 and John 20.[8]

All these women extended the mission of God in their unique callings of leadership. What would it be like if all these women weren't faithful in their callings simply because they—or others—believed their gender excluded them from leading people closer to the heart of God?

After all this study, it was impossible for us to say confidently that it is a universal principle that God does not desire women to be in leadership. It was clearly not the case. If these women are exceptions to a universal rule, then at least we know there are exceptions. It really hit home for us when we began to ask ourselves, "If Deborah, Phoebe, Priscilla, Huldah or Junia were members of our church, what would we tell them? Would we tell them to sit on the sidelines of ministry and ask them to refrain from using their gifts of teaching and leadership and oversight simply because of their gender?"

For us, telling a woman who is qualified that she cannot lead because of her gender did not seem consistent with the heart of God and his mission in our time and place. And with that realization, we became open to women in leadership in our community if God put them there. We now believe that if God were laying down an absolute law in the New Testament and backing it up by the order of creation, he would have been a little more consistent in his application of the principle throughout the narrative of Scripture.

FIRST TIMOTHY 2

Of course we had to deal specifically with 1 Timothy 2:11-12, which seemingly bars women from leadership in the church. On that, it's necessary to place it within the larger context of 1 Timothy 2, particularly what comes after it at the end of the chapter ("But women will be saved through childbearing," v. 15).

Paul was correcting a heresy in the early church. As it is translated in English and without an understanding of the culture in which it was written, it's hard to see. Taken literally, as translated, you have to say that women are saved by means of having children. However, Paul was correcting a group of protognostic heretics who said that women were the cause of man's fall and that God was displeased with them. They believed that in order to be saved, they needed to give up their sexuality, a source of temptation for men, and become more like what really pleases God—namely, men. In fact, the gnostic Gospel of Thomas (which seems to be full of the ideas Paul wanted to correct) records this: "Simon Peter said, 'Let Mary leave us, for women are not worthy of life.' Jesus said, 'I myself shall lead her in order to make her male so that she too may become a living spirit resembling you males. For every woman who will make herself male will enter the kingdom of heaven'" (Gospel of Thomas 114).

The idea that Paul was correcting was that only by giving up intercourse and other "worldly" pleasures can women (and men, but *especially* women) be saved. And if a woman had a child?

Well, how evil to take part in sex and bring another person into this wicked world! Clearly, this group didn't last long.

Women can be saved through (not "by means of," but "through the middle of"—that is, in spite of the experience of; the Greek can mean either) childbearing if they continue, like anyone else in faith (which saves you), love (which demonstrates you are saved) and holiness.

The last part of that paragraph is correcting a heresy (actually *raising* women's status) and is notoriously difficult to understand in English without a proper cultural background. It helps us to see that the verse we get so hung up on ("I do not permit a woman to teach or to have authority over a man"), which seems so clear in English, might fall into the same category.

First Timothy was written to a pastor (Timothy) in Ephesus, a center for the worship of the goddess Artemis. The word translated "exercise authority" appears only here in Scripture, so it's hard to get a handle on. It could mean "dominate" or "exercise authority in a domineering way." It seems that in Ephesus, where people were coming out of pagan goddess worship, women, feeling their newfound freedom in Christ, were taking a dominating attitude, claiming a privileged position.[9] Paul said they, like anyone else, should learn from their teachers quietly and submissively; he did not permit women to teach men in a domineering way.

Paul then corrected another heresy that was circulating, taught by the Sophists in a culture that was accustomed to goddess worship: that it wasn't Eve that sinned first, but Adam, and that in fact she was the one created first. It's foolish of us to get caught up in the "who sinned first" argument. Paul wasn't basing a prohibition of women in leadership on the order of creation; rather, he was reminding them of the facts of the biblical narrative and asking them to keep it straight. He was dealing with an early form of extreme religious feminism.

In essence, Paul wrote, "I don't allow women to dominate men, and these ideas going around are incorrect. Eve was the one who sinned first and wasn't the one created first. But, lest you think I buy into the other side that says women are evil, let me correct that as well." In light of Paul's admonition that, in Christ, there is neither male nor female, Jew nor Greek, slave nor free—and because we see the arc of Scripture (the way women's status is progressively raised through Scripture as well as many of the examples of women in leadership), we are hesitant to exclude women from any role, including that of elder.

How Might This Affect You in Your Church?

If you come from a tradition that excludes women from leadership and choose to take that position yourselves, embodying a missional orientation in your communities will be difficult. Don't discount this issue's importance in the minds of those you are trying to reach. Saying, for example, "We love homosexuals and invite them into our community, though we still adhere to a biblical ethic of sexuality and encourage all who come to embrace it" is one thing. Saying, "We withhold positions of leadership from some based on their gender" is another. Both statements will cost you, but we believe one is an issue of sin while the other is an issue of polity. In other words, if we handle the first incorrectly, we risk leading people into what Scripture clearly (in our minds) labels sin. If we do the second wrongly, we risk ordering our church in a way that might be less than biblical, but not—as far as we understand Scripture—sinful.

That being said, we encourage you to at least engage this issue on an elder level. I know a number of churches that have seen the importance of the issue and chosen to take it head on with their leadership team. Some have changed their position, as we did; some have modified it slightly; and some have remained the same. It is interesting to note that none that I have communicated with have regretted the engagement. Reading books together, praying over a pressing doctrinal issue and discussing the ethos and practice of your church will always be beneficial for your elder team.

There *are* some wrong reasons to have women as elders, such as having a token female presence on your elder team to appease a particular contingency in your church, to make a statement or to respond to pressure from the culture. We do believe it is the right thing to do, but we don't want anyone to do the right thing for the wrong reasons. In the same way, we believe there are wrong reasons to restrict women from your elder teams. Fear of people leaving your church is a significant one. There is fear in any change we might make, but through courageously facing issues liked these, we are formed as leaders. Similarly, if not having women in leadership is simply your de facto position and you've never explored the issue in depth with a thorough study on both sides of the issue, we don't believe that suffices. Your community deserves leaders who have thoughtfully and prayerfully engaged with this issue.

Throughout the entire scope and sweep of Scripture, it is difficult to find evidence that God restricts certain gifts along gender lines. Nowhere in Scripture do we see even a suggestion that this might be so.[10] Yet we know numerous talented female leaders who have been hurt, shunned or limited by the traditional stance simply because of their gender. The story of Acts is one of a gospel that included unlikely people in God's redemptive story, shocking those in the first century and even those in the early church. Some women in your church are gifted communicators; allow them to teach. Some are gifted leaders; allow them to lead. Unlocking the missional potential of your community will be infinitely easier when everyone in your church community is invited to use their God-given gifts to their fullest extent.

New movements of God's Spirit need to be put into new structures. Structures must always submit to the Spirit—even if or when the Spirit runs contrary to how we've always operated or what we've been told. As we join God's movement led by God's Spirit, the local church should actively seek out those who are qualified to lead the body of Christ faithfully and obediently toward God's purposes. People ask us, "Should women be in leadership?" and our response is always the same: "Leaders should be in leadership." Excluding women from leadership based solely on gender is unwise and, we believe, biblically unfounded.

Conversely, putting a women in a place of leadership simply because she is a woman is unwise. Often churches want to "make a statement" about women in ministry and place females in leadership when they are not gifted to lead. This has caused incredible relational, spiritual and organizational harm. Putting females in positions where they are not gifted does a disservice to the individual, the elder team, women in general and the church as a whole.

In summary, a person should be disqualified from leadership because of poor character or a lack of gifts, not because of gender. Only gifted and qualified leaders—regardless of gender—should serve as elders in local church settings. If you look at your church community for the kinds of wise, shepherding people you want on your elder team, you might find among them godly, qualified women who will be a blessing to your community and ultimately to the world.

12

Practical Questions and Answers

⫸

Paul gives the characteristics and roles of an elder, but he doesn't give exact details on how the elder process should occur. He desires for each congregation to seek the Spirit's guidance in a particular community to discern together what faithful participation in God's mission looks like. It is *freedom of form*.

The rhythms, practices and expressions specific to one context may be completely ineffective and irrelevant in another context. Listening to the Spirit, to the context and to your own church community are crucial. And wisdom is needed. We see Paul offering shrewd instruction to local communities; often the instructions are different in expression from one church to another. Elders rooted in the Father's mission need to ask God regularly to provide the wisdom needed by the local church leadership.

Below we seek to answer frequently asked questions about eldership.

Q: How Old Should Elders Be?

The apostle Paul offered no specific age requirement for elders. The only timeline he gave was that elders should not be new converts (but even that does not have a specific timeframe attached). Though in the Old Testament village elders were in their old age, elders within a church community were not required to be old. Paul's well-known words to Timothy apply: "Don't let anyone look down on you because you are young, but set an example for the believers in speech, in life, in love, in faith and in purity" (1 Timothy 4:12). Notice again that Paul was more concerned with character than anything else. He was not concerned that Timothy was young, but that he modeled a way of life in five distinct expressions.

The issue of character is more important than year of birth. Consider asking,

- Is this person spiritually mature?

- Does he meet the biblical qualifications?

- How has she exhibited godly character over a long, observable period?

- Will people in the church respect his leadership based on his character?[1]

If your context allows, we suggest a mix of generations that represents your church body and provides a broad perspective when making decisions together. Sometimes older-generation elders need to wrestle with new ideas and expressions of what participating in God's mission could look like. Newer-generation elders need to be reminded of what rootedness and faithfulness look like over a long period. Simply having one generational outlook in a church can limit perspective and result in a narrow expression of mission. A wide spread of ages also models to the entire church that generational variety is important and that no generational group is overrepresented.

A multigenerational group of elders may also help prevent generational divisions from occurring. Too many churches are stuck in old-guard versus new-guard issues. If a generationally diverse elder team can model unity and focus by remaining on mission, it will help the entire congregation follow suit. Keep in mind, however, that while no age is given in Scripture, knowing the context and culture of your church is important. Age may become a factor (though not the primary one) in determining which people are chosen as elders.

Q: HOW MANY ELDERS SHOULD OUR CHURCH HAVE?

The answer to this question falls into the freedom of form category. It is better to have a smaller number of qualified elders than a larger number of those about whom you are unsure. Logistically, having a small elder team seems to make sense for many churches. We know of a large church in the Northeast that had almost sixty elders. Attempting to match up everyone's schedules to attend an elder meeting was nearly impossible, and much of the pastor's time was spent in one-on-one appointments each month, updating the elders who missed the previous elder meetings. Additionally, it is difficult for elders to know one another and be involved in each other's lives when the numbers are too high.

Some churches have a set number of elders established in their constitution. Others have a ratio (for example, one elder for forty or fifty congregants). We would advise against establishing a hard and fast rule—either by number or ratio—for several reasons.

- The needs of the congregation are often based on the size of the congregation. As numbers grow, the dynamics of the congregation change.

- The types of elders and their gifts, passions and availability vary. The types of people the Spirit brings to your church will impact how oversight and shepherding need to occur.

- An established number of elders places too strong of an emphasis on a manmade structure and not enough on seeking the Spirit's guidance for who should lead the church.

Keep in mind that the larger the number of elders the more slowly decision making occurs. While efficiency is not the primary goal of an elder team, a top-heavy team can have a painstakingly slow decision-making process that can weigh a congregation down, erode trust and limit adaptability in following the Spirit. Although there may be a primary pastor who is most visible, communicates and teaches most often, and devotes a significant amount of time to the task of operating the church, he can lead with the confidence of knowing that the elders stand behind him in the vision.

In our (J.R.'s) church, we have had between five and seven elders at any given time. This has been a healthy number for our context, as scheduling meetings is not difficult and pursuing relational depth is natural. Our practical recommendation is to have an elder team large enough to provide appropriate and adequate oversight of a church but small enough to fit into a living room.

Q: SHOULD CHURCH STAFF BE INCLUDED ON THE ELDER TEAM? IF SO, HOW MANY?

Not all staff members should be elders and not all elders should be staff members, but some staff members should be elders.[2] Pastors on staff will have more of a pulse of the day-to-day elements and operations of the church itself, so they can update the elders on situations or people in the church. Also, unpaid elders are able to provide an outside perspective that is helpful for paid staff elders.

A word of caution: Refrain from emphasizing the dichotomy between paid elders and unpaid elders. Language creates culture. While there is a distinction regarding salary, and how and where time is spent in a given week or month, there is no distinction regarding authority among elders. Never create a wedge in the minds of the people in your church that paid elders are more important than unpaid elders. You are elders—together—leading the church, though with different levels of responsibility. Also be careful with your language; simply refer to the team as elders—without further titles or descriptive differentiators. If a distinction must be made, it would be wise to refer to them as staff elders and nonstaff elders.

My (J.R.'s) job description, which developed in partnership with our elders, includes leading our elder team and planning our elder meeting agendas and rhythms, but together we lead the church. I may initiate most of the content of our meetings, but I never make a significant decision outside the team—nor would I want to. This is how we interpret the principle of "first among equals." Though I initiate many things, ultimately I am accountable to them. They have the authority to fire me, confront me and reprimand me if need be, but together we lead the church.

By having both staff and nonstaff elders, our church has learned that leadership is not professional—done only by paid experts or the seminary trained. It also reminds us we are all a royal priesthood with the Spirit of God inside of each one of us. And it sends an important message about leadership: character and calling matter more than salary and education.

Additionally, if your elders also serve in a legal or other official capacity on a board of directors in your church, the IRS has requirements for nonprofit organizations receiving tax exemption regarding the ratio of paid to unpaid board members. It would be wise to look into this issue and all requirements, as tax laws change each year.

Q: How Often Should Elder Meetings Occur?

No set amount of time or frequency is given in Scripture. Meeting frequently can provide elders with a good pulse of the life the church and deepen relationships among them, but can also burden and exhaust your elders, especially nonstaff elders who have various other responsibilities outside the church. However, meeting too seldom can leave significant gaps in the shepherding and oversight of the congregation. This can leave the church feeling as though the elders are only symbolic representatives who loosely oversee the church without investing much time in the story, the mission and the lives of its people.

Here are questions that may help you and your elders determine an appropriate rhythm and frequency for your meetings:

- What is needed to get a sufficient read on our congregation in order to provide oversight and shepherding of the people entrusted to us?
- What would be too taxing or burdensome for us?
- What rhythm would leave us out of the loop or would provide unhealthy gaps in the system?
- Are there appropriate ways to update the elders or bring them up to speed in ways outside elder meetings (such as emails, phone calls, one-on-one meetings or lunches)?
- How can we ensure we have high-quality, unrushed time together in order to make sure the agenda doesn't squeeze out relational connection and prayer?

We've found the balance by holding an elder meeting one evening every other week, with each meeting lasting approximately two hours. We believed that every week would be overkill and would tax our elders too much, while meeting only once a month would be too infrequent (especially if an elder missed a meeting, which would leave two months until the last time we were all together). Since all of our elders know we meet every other Wednesday night, elders and their families can schedule that plan for them months in advance. Occasionally meetings are rescheduled to other days of the week (or pushed back a week) if there are a few people who will be absent (such as for summer vacations, business trips, illness). But, for the most part, we stick to every other Wednesday evening.

Q: What Should Elder Meetings Look Like?

Before deciding on the particulars of your elder meetings, it is important to remember the roles of elders: *shepherding, overseeing, teaching, equipping and modeling.* The elders' roles, functions and responsibilities determine the specific form of elder meetings. We strongly advise that meetings do not have a corporate board meeting feel. Do not forget: we are not called to maintain a religious organization; we are called *to nurture, shepherd and oversee* the lives of the flock entrusted to us. Roberts' Rules of Order do not apply.

Certainly, at times, elder meetings require significant operational decisions (such as hiring or firing staff, salaries, event logistics, budget approval, discerning future teaching series) that must not be neglected. However, all of these are rooted in guiding us into deeper participation with the ministry of Christ. Decisions should not be made in haste or taken lightly. However, business items on the agenda should not dominate elders meetings either. If elders get bogged down in the minutiae of church life, we can easily neglect the most important issues at hand.

Churches cannot afford to major in the minors and minor in the majors. Issues that do not relate to the overall culture, mission, direction or philosophy of the church should be given to other trustworthy, wise and spiritually mature leaders or deacons in the church to deal with outside the elder meeting. Quite simply, minimize—or eliminate—intramural decisions and discussions in your elder meetings.

So, what are the issues of greatest significance? We offer the following process and submit it for your consideration. Again, the purpose is not to provide a template, but to help assist you in providing helpful direction in order to stay focused.

1. Scripture and prayer. Adequate, unrushed time should be built into elder meetings for pursuing God's Word and God's heart. This is much more than simply reading a few verses and opening with a "word of prayer" before we start. It is seeking God's heart together and allowing him to guide our decisions, grant us wisdom, give us clear thinking in decision making, unify our team and deepen our faith individually and as a church.

2. Relational connection. Spending time in relationship with one another is crucial to unity and living life authentically and in a unified manner. We suggest building in time to ask how each of us is doing, along with an update on our families. This can be a rich time of sharing burdens and joys, hardships and successes with those you lead and serve alongside.

3. Updates. Because staff elders/pastors usually have a clear picture of the church due to their up-close involvement in the day-to-day operations, we suggest a regular, brief update of key issues, concerns and situations. Since shepherding the flock is a key role for elders, this time should include updating them about specific individuals or families within the congregation who are hurting and in need of extra care as well as those who are showing growth in their walk with Christ. Sometimes these updates can be given briefly via email or in the agenda sent out before the day of an elder meeting.

4. Key decisions. We have already addressed decision making within an elder team in a previous chapter, so not much explanation is required. Allowing time to discuss these decisions, assess implications and ask questions for clarification is crucial to making wise decisions.

5. *Focused time to gain perspective.* Again, there is no set directive regarding this element of a meeting, but it can be easy for elder meetings to look only at the immediate issues that face a church. It is important to maintain perspective to take a broader and longer view of the church in assessing direction and expressions—and if those expressions are moving in a healthy trajectory of God's general and specific call on the congregation. Here are a few good questions to consider discussing in meetings:

- What season do we sense our church is in right now?

- What do we sense God calling our church to be a part of in the next six months? Twelve months? Three years?

- In what ways is our church healthy? In what ways is it lacking health?

- Who has God brought to us in this season of our church? How can we care for, equip, shepherd and teach effectively and faithfully with what we know now?

- What factors are keeping our church from joining with God more faithfully and loving others more compassionately? How can we challenge, encourage, train and equip toward greater faithfulness and commitment to Jesus?

- What sacrifices do we sense God is calling us to make or in what ways is God asking for deepened faith from us as we move into the future?

- If Paul wrote a letter to our local church—even to us as elders—like he did to those in Asia Minor, what do we think he might say?

- What do we sense the Spirit's intent is for our church?

6. *Additional elements.* Leave a time for elders to bring up other elements during meetings. There may be something an elder is thinking through—an encouraging thought, a concern or even a word from the Lord—that needs to be voiced or addressed. This may include a previous thought or one that surfaced at some point during the meeting. Allowing space for this to occur can allow for further ownership and space to acknowledge and address issues that relate to the overall spiritual health of your church.

A few days before an elder meeting, I (J.R.) check with our other pastor/staff elder to see if there are items that should be included on the elder agenda. I then email the agenda to the elder team about a day before our scheduled meeting so they can read it over, think about what we will be discussing and print off a copy to bring to the meeting. In addition to the agenda, I secure our meeting location.

Also, before each meeting, I ask a different elder to lead our time in Scripture and in prayer. We leave it up to the elder to share whatever Scripture passage he desires (often it is a passage through which the Lord has met him during a recent time in the Word). Sometimes an elder will share a short reflection, offer a series of reflection questions about the passage, lead us in *lectio divina* or pray the passage itself.

Q: WHERE SHOULD MEETINGS BE HELD?

Deciding where elder meetings should take place is another example of freedom of form. Location matters—and the locations of elder meetings are no exception. Ultimately, elder meetings can be held just about anywhere, but elders should be thoughtful in choosing a location. Find a place that is relationally oriented but relatively distraction-free.

We encourage you to avoid meeting in a location that feels like a corporate boardroom. Being in such a setting can reinforce the mindset that elders are to act as the board of directors, to managing an organization instead of living out our calling to join in God's mission together as his people. For churches with their own facilities, it may be wise to meet in the church building—or it may be wise to meet offsite. Meeting in a restaurant or coffee shop may help your elders think more like missionaries and consider the mission field outside the four walls of your church. One church I know holds its elder meetings in a pub to remind them that their church is intended to love the people of their community. However, if you are going to be spending considerable time in prayer during your meetings or are dealing with sensitive information, you will most likely need more privacy and less noise, thus limiting your options.[3]

Our elder meetings have been held in various places but almost always happen in an elder's home, usually rotating among elders. Being in someone's home is a great way to get to know them, their family and their story. A South African pastor friend of mine once told me, "You really don't know someone until you've been in their kitchen." If elders are hospitable, as is one of the biblical qualifications, opening up homes should be a normal part of their rhythm. Regardless of where you meet, make sure you are purposeful about the location, and consider how it may shape your thoughts about mission.

Q: What Role Do Elders Play Within a Sunday Service? What Role Do Elders Play Throughout the Week?

Paul did not give us explicit instructions for what role an elder should play when the body gathers. He said that an elder should be able to teach, but did not imply that this be entirely in an upfront capacity. In fact, in some cases, that may seem forced or may put a large burden on nonstaff elders. However, if the elders are to be the shepherds, teachers, overseers, equippers and modelers of the congregation, being absent from gathered congregational life would seem unwise.

Be purposeful in having your elders involved in your gatherings—both up front and behind the scenes, and in official and unofficial capacities. If elders lead only in official capacities up front, the congregation may believe they are not among the people. It is important elders have various areas of involvement (including simply attending with their families) so that they model what healthy involvement in shepherding a community looks like. Some elders may have more active roles on a particular Sunday than others, but both are important. Elders do not have to carry significant responsibilities during weekend services, but it is important to communicate deliberately to your church that the elder team shepherds and oversees the church in partnership with the pastoral staff.

Q: How Much Authority Should Elders Have in a Local Church?

Scripturally, it is clear that elders have authority in the church, but Paul does not spell out exactly *how much* authority elders should have. This is another opportunity to exercise wisdom. Talking regularly and openly with elders and staff about this is crucial. It may even change in different seasons of the life of a local congregation. Certain seasons may call for more authority to be exercised and others may call for less. This must be discerned in prayer and within the community itself.

Trust and authority are precious commodities. If used too forcibly, authority can crush the spirits and increase suspicion in the hearts and minds of congregants. Too little authority marked by timidity or apathy confuses congregations, can erode confidence in the leaders of the church and often leads to feelings of anxiety. Elders should lead in such a way that those they lead gladly follow (see Hebrews 13:17; 1 Corinthians 16:15-16; 1 Peter 5:5). People should not submit to elders simply because they have the title of elder. People will be more willing to submit when their elders' lives are a model of maturity in Christ and because they have the responsibility to shepherd, guide, instruct and lead the congregation faithfully and diligently.

Epilogue

Eldership as Stewardship

᠊ᥬᥨ᠊

Paul writes that elders are God's stewards (Titus 1:7). Elders take what God has entrusted to them and care for it as best they can. Exemplifying what a biblical community looks like by modeling a healthy microcommunity is essential to God-honoring stewardship. We strive to cultivate a culture where the kingdom of God is imagined, embraced and expressed—and where people are flourishing as they are rooted in Christ.

The sacred calling of an elder is not a charge to do what every other church is doing. It is not a call to maintain the status quo or to preserve the past. No, it is to join God in the here and now and to live that out obediently in our unique context. It is to plead, urge, love, encourage and challenge people to participate in the work of Christ's ministry. May we strive to know God, to steward faithfully who and what has been entrusted to us and to be unified in our pursuit of the Father's heart.

As an elder rooted in Christ, guided by the Spirit and committed to God and his mission,

May you oversee the people entrusted to your care with wisdom.

May you shepherd the flock with compassion.

May you teach the truth of God's story with conviction.

May you equip God's people with courage.

May you humbly model to others what participation with God and his mission looks like.

And may it be met with these words from the Father: "Well done, good and faithful servant."

Discussion Questions

CHAPTER 1: MISSION-ORIENTED ELDERS

1. As you think about the nature of this chapter and your current church context, what are you feeling?

2. What might "sending capacity over seating capacity" look like in your church on a practical level? What sacrifices would have to be made if that were to become an even higher priority?

3. If your elders were to bet the farm on discipleship in your church, what might that look like?

4. What element listed in this chapter has the greatest potential to derail mission in your church? How might you address it now? If left unchecked, what impact might it have on your church?

CHAPTER 2: CHARACTERISTICS OF MISSION ALIGNMENT—AND WHAT DERAILS IT

1. Do your structures facilitate healthy processes, or are they stuck in the cogs of bureaucracy?

2. What is your church's leadership posture? Does it maintain the status quo or unleash people into new realms of possibility? In what ways?

3. David Allen said, "Pay attention to what you are paying attention to." What are your elders paying attention to the most? Are you satisfied with that answer? What sorts of things need more attention?

4. What is your theology of change for the sake of mission? What is your theology of risk? Of failure?

5. Where does leadership end and manipulation begin?

Chapter 3: The Roles of an Elder

1. When you think about elder meetings, how do you feel? What adjectives come to mind? What factors contribute to your response?

2. If you have yet to have elder meetings, what words would you use to describe your future elders meetings?

3. What are the areas of deepest concern and deepest excitement as you think about eldership?

4. Why do you think Paul was so adamant about an elder structure within the local church setting?

5. How might an elder team help your church remain faithful to Jesus?

6. If eldership is about stewardship, how are the leaders of your church doing with what has been entrusted to them by God?

7. What might you need to unlearn—and relearn—regarding the role of the church? The mission of God? The role of an elder?

Chapter 4: Biblical Qualifications for an Elder

1. Think about your elders. What is the congregation's perception of their level of character? How might you know if that perception is accurate?

2. Why do you think Paul cares so much about the character of elders?

3. What might occur in your church if leaders who were not biblically qualified became elders?

4. Which of the biblical qualifications is most difficult for you to adhere to personally? Why? Which is most difficult to judge in your own life? In the lives of others?

5. Do you think it is possible to overemphasize the biblical qualifications for eldership? If so, how might we know?

6. What might be a wise way to assess the character of elders in relation to these specific qualifications?

7. In what specific situations might elders need to operate as red blood cells, and in what situations would they need to act as white blood cells? How will you discern the difference?

8. Which of these qualifications is most often overlooked, undervalued or forgotten? Why?

9. Why is a willingness to serve crucial for an elder? What might it look like if an elder was unwilling to serve wholeheartedly? How should that be addressed?

Chapter 5: Cultivating an Ethos Rooted in God's Mission

1. What are elements or characteristics of the ethos of your church? What does your congregation care most about? How might you find that out?

2. In what ways is the ethos of your church revealed in the hearts and stories of your elders?

3. Peter Drucker wrote, "The purpose of management of the church is not to make it more businesslike but to make it more churchlike." Does this resonate with you? If so, how?

4. What have been the most formidable events and shaping experiences in the life of your church, both good and bad? What

stories are considered legend? What might that reveal about who you are and what you care about?

5. What problems are worth creating if it helps challenge the status quo? What sacred cows might need to be slaughtered? At what cost will that happen, and is it worth it for the sake of God's mission?

6. Why have you chosen to do church in the manner in which you are doing it? What are the core motivations behind the way you are doing church? How many of them are non-negotiable?

7. In Acts 10–11, the leaders of the early church faced a significant paradigm shift when Peter experienced the dream of unkosher animals being lowered on a sheet. What if God did something powerful and undeniable in your church that was counter to your tradition, doctrine or denominational mandates? What would you do?

Chapter 6: Selecting Elders

1. If you are in a church plant, why might someone who has been an elder in a past church not necessarily fit as an elder in yours?

2. Do you think term limits for elders is healthy or unhealthy? What do you see as the benefits and liabilities?

3. After reading this chapter, has your view of selecting/electing elders been changed in any way? How do your views fit with your denomination or church tradition in this respect?

4. How do you think the views and voices of your congregation should be included in selecting elders?

5. Will you install elders in your church? How? Do you feel the topic of eldership is given enough weight? Not enough?

6. How will you handle people who express a desire to be an elder in your community? How about people who feel entitled to be an elder?

7. What's your roadmap for developing people you think will make good elders in the future, though they aren't ready yet?

8. What questions do you have that you feel should be asked in every potential elder interview?

Chapter 7: Eldership as Spiritual Formation

1. How important are elders to the overall spiritual health of a local church? How might your church suffer spiritually if your elders were unhealthy?

2. How are you as elders growing to become more like Christ because of your role?

3. We mentioned three significant temptations. Which one of these do you find yourself wrestling with most often? What circumstances bring about these temptations strongly?

4. What do you think of the concept of self-differentiation? Where do you see this in the life and ministry of Jesus? In the words and actions of the apostles in the book of Acts?

5. Be honest: do you feel responsible *for* your church and its members or do you feel responsible *to* them? How might you and your elders think and lead differently if you all saw yourselves as being responsible *to* those in your church and not responsible *for* them?

6. What are some difficulties you have faced as a church that have led to maturity both on your elder team and corporately as a church? What are some you are going through right now that might have the same effect?

7. How do we call each other to a radical minimum standard of disciplines and spiritual life as elders? How might that impact the church at large, directly and indirectly?

8. Do the people in your church know how to experience God together? As individuals? How are you demonstrating this as elders?

Chapter 8: Team Leadership

1. What do you think about the polycentric approach to leadership?

2. How would your church know if you are person oriented or team oriented in your approach to church leadership? How would the congregation answer that question?

3. As you think about the five giftings and your elder team, where are you strongest? Where are you weakest? What implications has that had on the overall culture and emphasis of your church—and what do you think should be done about it moving forward?

4. If your team were to move more in the direction of team-oriented leadership and decision making, what would have to change? What would have to be sacrificed? How would this approach make your leadership more robust and more focused for rallying around God's mission more effectively?

5. Why is being a healthy "community within a community" so important for an elder team? What could you do to enhance community on your elder team?

6. If a healthy team-oriented approach among the elders was implemented in your church, how might that express a healthy understanding of the body of Christ at work?

7. How and where does your church communicate the importance of everyone's giftings rather than just a handful of leaders or pastors?

CHAPTER 9: THE ROLE OF ELDERS IN DECISION MAKING

1. How would you evaluate your community and yourself as a leader on the three issues of listening to the Spirit, listening to Scripture and listening to each other? In which are you strongest? Weakest?

2. As a leader, how do you respond to the word *consensus*? Why?

3. How are the majority of decisions made in your church? Why? If you sense a lack of balance between the congregation making decisions, the elders making recommendations and the elders making decisions for the community, what steps might you take to move your community's decision-making processes toward a better balance?

4. Think about some of the significant decisions that need to be made in your church. Which category does each decision need to be put into: communal, elder recommendations or elder decisions? How will you know?

5. What is your church's understanding of and trust level with the Holy Spirit? With leadership and elders? What might need to change in order to listen more attentively as spiritual overseers?

6. What are ways you can build bridges of trust with your congregation through communication and decision making?

7. How might you work out the balance between a biblical understanding of leadership in the church and a biblical understanding of the priesthood of all believers?

8. How can your church ensure decisions are being made with proper motives among your leaders and the congregation?

CHAPTER 10: THE DIFFICULT TASKS OF ELDERS

1. What are some of the most difficult tasks you've experienced—or that you anticipate experiencing—in your church? How have you handled them? How might you be better equipped to handle them in the future?

2. Can you think of a time when your elders handled a difficult situation wisely and compassionately? In what specific ways was it handled?

3. Can you think of a time when your elders handled a difficult situation poorly? How might you have handled it better?

4. What is your "theology of conflict"? When conflict arises, what are you tempted to believe about the health of your church or the nature of people? Is it biblically accurate?

5. In what area(s) might you, the other elders or people in your church be most vulnerable currently? Where might you need to provide more protection in that vulnerability?

6. How will your elder team handle couples in your community living together without the benefit of marriage? What about when one or both are spiritually seeking but not yet self-identifying as Christians?

7. When was the last time you as an elder team gathered to lay hands on and pray for a member of your community? What holds you back from doing so?

CHAPTER 11: WHAT ABOUT WOMEN ELDERS?

1. What is your traditional or denominational stance on women

in church leadership? Have you as an elder team considered women in leadership? Do you know how each member of your elder team feels about the issue?

2. If you were to include gifted women leaders on your elder team, what implications might that have on your church? On the elder team?

3. Should husbands and wives serve on the same leadership team? Why or why not? What might be the benefits and drawbacks?

4. If Deborah, Phoebe, Huldah, Priscilla or Junia were a part of your church, what would you tell them about leadership? Why?

5. Are there women in your church gifted in leadership? Are they being affirmed, encouraged, supported, equipped and unleashed in their giftedness? How might *they* answer that question?

6. How often does your church hear from the pulpit the stories of faith-filled women found throughout Scripture?

7. If Jesus were in your church now and you asked him about the issue of women in leadership, what do you think he might say? Why do you think that?

8. How can this issue be communicated to your church in a way that is clearly biblical and not interpreted as someone's "agenda"?

Acknowledgments

J.R. Briggs

Thanks to Bob Hyatt for hatching this idea on a warm spring afternoon in the garden at Richmond Hill. I am thankful for your ongoing friendship and partnership in the gospel.

Thanks to Doug and Mear Moister, Duane and Ang Freed, Tim and Cindy Culp, and Dennis and Claudia Brice for your rugged commitment to Jesus and The Renew Community.

Thanks to the multitude of pastors and elders who provided crucial feedback and shared stories of their experiences throughout the writing process. Your involvement helped to make this book more robust and clear.

Thanks to Al Hsu and the InterVarsity Press team for your continued commitment to developing resources—including this one—to equip the body of Christ.

Thanks to Andrew Wolgemuth, for your expertise, encouragement and friendship in this writing journey.

Thanks to Megan for your commitment to travel this road with me. Through the twists and turns, I'm glad you're by my side.

And thanks to Jesus, who, being the perfect Head, extends outlandish grace by calling imperfect people like us to be a part of his body—and be on mission in the world.

Bob Hyatt

I want to thank my wife, Amy, for being an instrumental part of my story, both in planting our church, Evergreen, and in life. God has used you in my life and in the lives of countless others. Thank you for being open to the Spirit and to serving God together.

Thanks to J.R. Briggs for listening to this idea and saying yes. And thanks for being the organized one.

Thank you to Andrew Wolgemuth and Al Hsu for all your encouragement and wisdom in this process. Your expertise and input have been invaluable.

I'm especially indebted to the elders of Evergreen, past and present. Thank you to Dustin, Chris, Devin, Sarah, Tina, Mike, Brynn, Stephen, Chip, Brian, Johnny V. and Rich. Through good times and bad, you have always put the well-being of our community and the person of Jesus first and foremost.

And a special thank you to Dustin Bagby, who first suggested this idea to us.

Notes

Introduction: Structured for Mission

[1]Mike Breen writes about endoskeletons and exoskeletons in relation to churches in his book *Multiplying Missional Leaders,* Kindle edition.

[2]For more on the Ecclesia Network, see www.ecclesianet.org.

[3]See Graham Buxton, *Dancing in the Dark: The Privilege of Participating in the Ministry of Christ* (Milton Keynes, UK: Paternoster, 2001), p. xi.

Chapter 1: Mission-Oriented Elders

[1]Christopher J. H. Wright, *The Mission of God's People* (Grand Rapids: Zondervan, 2010), Kindle edition, loc. 3927.

[2]Ibid., loc. 4078.

[3]Christopher J. H. Wright, *The Mission of God: Unlocking the Bible's Grand Narrative* (Downers Grove, IL: IVP Academic, 2013), p. 62.

Chapter 2: Characteristics of Mission Alignment—and What Derails It

[1]Christopher J. H. Wright, *The Mission of God's People* (Grand Rapids: Zondervan, 2010), Kindle edition, loc. 4164.

[2]Ibid., loc. 4984.

[3]Alan Hirsch, *The Forgotten Ways* (Ada, MI: Brazos Press, 2009), p. 24.

[4]Lecture by Dallas Willard at the Ecclesia National Gathering, February 16, 2010, Chevy Chase, Maryland.

[5]Neil Cole, *Search and Rescue: Becoming a Disciple Who Makes a Difference* (Grand Rapids: Baker Books, 2008), p. 185.

[6]Lecture by Dallas Willard.

[7]Michael Frost and Alan Hirsch, *The Shaping of Things to Come* (Peabody, MA: Hendrickson Publishers, 2003), p. 189.

[8]Neil Cole, *Organic Leadership: Leading Naturally Right Where You Are* (Grand Rapids: Baker Books, 2010), p. 271.

Chapter 3: The Roles of an Elder

[1]Phil A. Newton, *Elders in Congregational Life: Rediscovering the Biblical Model for Church Leadership* (Grand Rapids: Kregel Publishing, 1995), Kindle edition, loc. 1115.

[2]Benjamin Merkle, *40 Questions About Elders and Deacons* (Grand Rapids: Kregel Publishing, 2007), Kindle edition, loc. 69.

[3]Ibid., loc. 550.

[4]Gene Getz, *Elders and Leaders: God's Plan for Leading the Church—A Biblical, Historical and Cultural Perspective* (Chicago: Moody Publishing, 2003), Kindle edition, loc. 2610.

[5]In some traditions, priests are called presbyters.

[6]Newton, *Elders in Congregational Life*, loc. 709.

[7]Getz, *Elders and Leaders*, loc. 2427.

[8]Joseph Umidi, *Transformational Coaching: Bridge Building That Impacts, Connects, and Advances the Ministry and the Marketplace* (Maitland, FL: Xulon Press, 2005), p. 11.

Chapter 4: Biblical Qualifications for an Elder

[1]These three categories come from Benjamin Merkle, *Why Elders?* (Grand Rapids: Kregel Publishing, 2009), p. 67.

[2]We are well aware that Paul's phrase "the husband of one wife" can be controversial in relation to women in church leadership. While we have committed a significant amount of time for rigorous study on this important issue and while we advocate for wise and faithful women in leadership positions, we know that not everyone holds this position. We will address this is greater depth in chapter 11.

[3]Joseph Umidi, *Transformational Coaching: Bridge Building That Impacts, Connects, and Advances the Ministry and the Marketplace* (Maitland, FL: Xulon Press, 2005), p. 114.

[4]Merkle, *Why Elders?* p. 37.

Chapter 5: Cultivating an Ethos Rooted in God's Mission

[1]For photos and more information, see "Ellen Phillips Samuel Memorial Sculpture Garden," Association for Public Arts, http://associationforpublicart .org/interactive-art-map/ellen-phillips-samuel-memorial-north-terrace.

[2]See "The Preacher," Association for Public Arts, http://associationforpub licart.org/interactive-art-map/the-preacher.

[3]Graham Buxton, *Dancing in the Dark: The Privilege of Participating in the Ministry of Christ* (Milton Keynes, UK: Paternoster, 2001), p. 88.

[4]Alan Hirsch, *The Forgotten Ways* (Grand Rapids: Baker Books, 2009), p. 197.

[5]For more information on this service, which tracks the websites visited on a computer, visit www.covenanteyes.com.

CHAPTER 6: SELECTING ELDERS

[1]A management team is similar to the provisional elder team we outlined above. But in our experience, a management team is often provided (without much input from the church planter) by the denomination or church-planting organization and is focused mainly on getting the church to sustainability. A provisional elder team acts more as a true elder team, having been invited by the church planter or new church community to speak into the life of the new congregation.

[2]Some suggest evaluations based on the four Cs: competency, character, chemistry and calling.

CHAPTER 7: ELDERSHIP AS SPIRITUAL FORMATION

[1]Richard Baxter, *The Reformed Pastor* (1657; republished Colorado Springs, CO: Multnomah Press, 1982), p. 21.

[2]Ibid.

[3]*Kairos* is a Greek word for time, which is different from the word *chronos*. Chronos is linear, calendar time, but kairos refers to significant moments and opportunities pregnant with possibility. In this usage, it refers to those times when God steps into chronos.

[4]Baxter, *The Reformed Pastor*, p. 21.

[5]Jim Herrington, R. Robert Creech and Trisha Taylor, *The Leader's Journey* (San Francisco: Jossey-Bass, 2003), p. 21.

[6]Dallas Willard, *The Spirit of the Disciplines* (San Francisco: HarperSan-Francisco, 1988), p. 9.

[7]Herrington, Creech and Taylor, *The Leader's Journey*, pp. 135-36.

CHAPTER 8: TEAM LEADERSHIP

[1]Or *pastors*—the word in the Greek is the same: *poimen.*

[2]JR Woodward, *Creating a Missional Culture* (Downers Grove, IL: Inter-Varsity Press, 2012), p. 92. A polycentric team is one in which all members share the "center," and no one personality is the central one.

[3]Alan Hirsch and Darryn Altclass, *The Forgotten Ways Handbook* (Grand Rapids: Brazos Press, 2009), p. 104.

[4]For a more thorough discussion of these giftings, see Michael Frost and Alan Hirsch, *The Shaping of Things to Come* (Peabody, MA: Hendrickson Publishers, 2003), or Mike Breen's *Building a Discipling Culture* (Pauleys Island, SC: 3 Dimension Ministries, 2009). Also see the free online APEST assessment tool at www.fivefoldsurvey.com.

[5]Phil A. Newton, *Elders in Congregational Life: Rediscovering the Biblical Model for Church Leadership* (Grand Rapids: Kregel Publishing, 1995), Kindle edition, loc. 611.

[6]Woodward, *Creating a Missional Culture,* p. 94.

CHAPTER 9: THE ROLE OF ELDERS IN DECISION MAKING

[1]Gailyn Van Rheenan, "Contrasting Missional and Church Growth Perspectives," *Restoration Quarterly* 48, no. 1 (2006): 225-32.

[2]Larry Julian, *God Is My Coach: A Business Leader's Guide to Finding Clarity in an Uncertain World* (New York: Center Street, 2009), p. xviii.

[3]Leonard Sweet and Frank Viola, *Jesus Manifesto* (Nashville: Thomas Nelson, 2010), p. 144.

[4]Craig Van Gelder, *The Ministry of the Missional Church* (Grand Rapids: Baker Books, 2007), Kindle edition, loc. 1521.

[5]Paul Anderson, "The Meeting for Worship in Which Business Is Conducted," *Quaker Religious Thought* 106-107 (November 2006): 26-47.

CHAPTER 10: THE DIFFICULT TASKS OF ELDERS

[1]Watch for men and women who watch members of the opposite sex a little too closely. Maybe they are lonely and looking for a relationship. But if you get the sense that they are making others uncomfortable, it's time for a sit-down. My (Bob's) wife has been invaluable in this respect; numerous times she has let me know about the guy rapidly gaining a reputation for lingering hugs or for eyes that didn't stay focused where they needed to be.

[2]Jesus' words in John 8:11 to the woman caught in adultery are instructive. "Neither do I condemn you. Go now and leave your life of sin." What a wonderful balance of love and encouragement to repentance and change!
[3]Whether this may be so or not theologically, it's almost never helpful to say this aloud to someone who is suffering.

CHAPTER 11: WHAT ABOUT WOMEN ELDERS?

[1]William Webb, *Slaves, Women and Homosexuals* (Downers Grove, IL: InterVarsity Press, 2009), p. 51.
[2]On the issue of homosexuality, Webb comes to the opposite conclusion: far from being a loosening of sexual ethics across the scope of Scripture, the movement goes the other way, from polygamy and other practices to "one man and one woman," a picture of Christ and his bride.
[3]N. T. Wright wrote, "We have our own clear but unstated rules about whose space is which; so did they. And Mary has just flouted them. *And Jesus declares that she is right to do so.* She is 'sitting at his feet'; a phrase that doesn't mean what it would mean today, the adoring student gazing up in admiration and love at the wonderful teacher. As is clear from the use of the phrase elsewhere in the NT (for instance, Paul with Gamaliel), to sit at the teacher's feet is a way of saying you are being a *student*, picking up the teacher's wisdom and learning; and in that practical world you wouldn't do this just for the sake of informing your own mind and heart, but in order to be a teacher, a rabbi, yourself. Like much in the Gospels, this story is left cryptic as far as we at least are concerned, but I doubt if any first-century reader would have missed the point." "Women's Service in the Church: The Biblical Basis," a conference paper for the symposium Men, Women and the Church, St John's College, Durham, UK, September 4, 2004.
[4]Scot McKnight, *Junia Is Not Alone* (Englewood, CO: Patheos Press, 2011), Kindle edition, loc. 84.
[5]Ibid.
[6]Ibid., loc. 98.
[7]For more on this, see *Junia Is Not Alone* by Scot McKnight.
[8]Kurt Willems, "N. T. Wright on Why Women SHOULD Be in Pastoral Roles," Patheos, www.patheos.com/blogs/thepangeablog/2012/08/06/n-t-wright-on-why-women-should-be-in-pastoral-roles/.

[9]Though definitely not the norm in Jewish culture, at least in Greco-Roman culture, women held places of authority in the religious world. "For example, while Paul was planting the Ephesus church, Iuliane served as high priestess of the imperial cult in Magnesia, a city fifteen miles from Ephesus. . . . The more Romanized the area, the more visible were women leaders." Ronald W. Pierce and Rebecca Merrill Groothius, eds., *Discovering Biblical Equality* (Downers Grove, IL: IVP Academic, 2005), p. 116.

[10]Dallas Willard wrote, "There is no suggestion whatsoever in scripture or the history of Christ's people that the gifts of the Spirit are distributed along gender lines. It is clearly something that does not even appear on the mental horizon of the inspired writers. And, if it had done so, can one even imagine that they would have failed to state it clearly? Especially if it is as important as those who oppose female leadership make it out to be. You have to put the fact that, in discussing the distribution and ministry of gifts by the Spirit, nothing is said about gender, down alongside that fact that many men are allowed to serve in official roles that manifestly are not supernaturally gifted. Then you realize that official leadership roles, as widely understood now, are as much human artifacts as they are a divine arrangement." In the foreword to Alan F. Johnson, *How I Changed My Mind About Women in Leadership* (Grand Rapids: Zondervan, 2010).

CHAPTER 12: PRACTICAL QUESTIONS AND ANSWERS

[1]Benjamin Merkle, *40 Questions About Elders and Deacons* (Grand Rapids: Kregel Publishing, 2007), Kindle edition, loc. 1132.

[2]For a more in-depth exploration of this question, see ibid., chap. 23.

[3]Bob's elder team likes to alternate meetings between a home and a pub for this reason. Home meetings tend to focus more on prayer, as the space is more conducive to that.

Recommended Resources

ELDERSHIP

Getz, Gene. *Elders and Leaders*. Chicago: Moody, 2003.

Merkle, Benjamin. *40 Questions About Elders and Deacons*. Grand Rapids: Kregel Publishing, 2007.

———. *Why Elders?* Grand Rapids: Kregel Publishing, 2009.

Newton, Phil A. *Elders in Congregational Life*. Grand Rapids: Kregel Publishing, 2005.

Strauch, Alexander. *Biblical Eldership*. Colorado Springs, CO: Lewis & Roth Publishers, 1997.

THE MISSION OF GOD AND THE MISSION OF THE CHURCH

Buxton, Graham. *Dancing in the Dark*. Carlisle, UK: Paternoster, 2001.

Guder, Darrell L., ed. *The Missional Church*. Grand Rapids: Eerdmans, 1998.

Hirsch, Alan, and Michael Frost. *The Shaping of Things to Come*. Ada, MI: Baker Books, 2003.

Keller, Timothy. *Center Church*. Grand Rapids: Zondervan, 2012.

McNeal, Reggie. *Missional Renaissance*. San Francisco: Jossey-Bass, 2009.

Newbigin, Lesslie. *Mission in Christ's Way*. New York: Friendship Press, 1988.

———. *The Open Secret*. Grand Rapids: Eerdmans, 1995.

Taylor, John V. *The Go-Between God*. Oxford, UK: Oxford University Press, 1979.

Woodward, JR. *Creating a Missional Culture*. Downers Grove, IL: InterVarsity Press, 2012.

Wright, Christopher J. H. *The Mission of God*. Downers Grove, IL: InterVarsity Press, 2006.

———. *The Mission of God's People*. Grand Rapids: Zondervan, 2010.

Pastoral Leadership

Barton, Ruth Haley. *Pursuing God's Will Together.* Downers Grove, IL: InterVarsity Press, 2012.

Baxter, Richard. *The Reformed Pastor.* Colorado Springs, CO: Multnomah Press, 1982.

Clinton, Robert. *The Making of a Leader.* Colorado Springs, CO: NavPress, 2012.

Griffith, James, and William Easum. *Ten Most Common Mistakes Made by New Church Starts.* Atlanta: Chalice Press, 2008.

Halter, Hugh, and Matt Smay. *AND.* Grand Rapids: Zondervan, 2010.

Hansen, David. *The Art of Pastoring.* Downers Grove, IL: InterVarsity Press, 2012.

Marshall, Colin, and Tony Payne. *The Trellis and the Vine.* Youngstown, OH: Matthias Media, 2009.

McManus, Erwin Raphael. *An Unstoppable Force.* Colorado Springs, CO: David C. Cook, 2013.

McNeal, Reggie. *The Present Future.* San Francisco: Jossey-Bass, 2009.

Nouwen, Henri J. M. *In the Name of Jesus.* Danvers, MA: Crossroad Publishing, 1992.

Peterson, Eugene. *Working the Angles.* Grand Rapids: Eerdmans, 1989.

Roberts, Bob, Jr. *The Multiplying Church.* Grand Rapids: Zondervan, 2008.

Roberts, Wes, and Glenn C. Marshall. *Reclaiming God's Original Intent for the Church.* Colorado Springs, CO: NavPress, 2004.

Sanders, J. Oswald. *Spiritual Leadership.* Chicago: Moody Publishers, 1974.

Stott, John R. W. *Problems of Christian Leadership.* Downers Grove, IL: InterVarsity Press, 2014.

———. *The Spirit, the Church, and the World.* Downers Grove, IL: InterVarsity Press, 1990.

Yeakley, Tom. *Growing Kingdom Character.* Colorado Springs, CO: NavPress, 2011.

Discipleship

Bonhoeffer, Dietrich. *The Cost of Discipleship.* New York: Scribner, 1963.

Foster, Richard J. *Prayer.* New York: HarperOne, 2002.

Hallesby, Ole. *Prayer.* Minneapolis: Augsburg, 1994.

Hirsch, Alan, and Debra Hirsh. *Untamed.* Ada, MI: Baker Books, 2010.

Murray, Andrew. *With Christ in the School of Prayer.* Alachua, FL: Bridge-Logos, 1999.

Vanier, Jean. *Community and Growth.* Mahwah, NJ: Paulist Press, 1989.

Willard, Dallas. *The Divine Conspiracy.* San Francisco: Harper, 1998.

———. *The Great Omission.* San Francisco: HarperOne, 2006.

WOMEN IN MINISTRY

Bristow, John T. *What Paul Really Said About Women: The Apostle's Liberating Views on Equality in Marriage, Leadership and Love.* San Francisco, CA: HarperOne, 1991.

Cunningham, Loren, David Joel Hamilton and Janice Rogers. *Why Not Women?* Seattle: YWAM Publishing, 2000.

James, Carolyn Custis. *Half the Church: Recapturing God's Global Vision for Women.* Grand Rapids: Zondervan, 2011.

Johnson, Alan F., ed. *How I Changed My Mind About Women in Leadership: Compelling Stories from Prominent Evangelicals.* Grand Rapids: Zondervan, 2010.

McKnight, Scot. *The Blue Parakeet.* Grand Rapids: Zondervan, 2003.

———. *Junia Is Not Alone.* Englewood, CO: Patheos Press (ebook), 2011.

Pierce, Ronald W., Rebecca Merrill Groothuis and Gordon D. Fee, eds. *Discovering Biblical Equality: Complementarity Without Hierarchy.* Downers Grove, IL: IVP Academic, 2005.

Sumner, Sarah. *Men and Women in the Church: Building Consensus on Christian Leadership.* Downers Grove, IL: InterVarsity Press, 2003.

Tucker, Ruth A., and Walter Liefeld. *Daughters of the Church: Women and Ministry from New Testament Times to the Present.* Grand Rapids: Zondervan, 1987.

Webb, William J. *Slaves, Women and Homosexuals.* Downers Grove, IL: InterVarsity Press, 2001.

Wright, N. T. *Surprised by Scripture.* San Francisco, CA: HarperOne, 2014.

About the Authors

J.R. Briggs has served in megachurch, church plant and house church contexts. He is the founding pastor and cultural cultivator of The Renew Community, a Jesus community for the hurting and the hungry in the northern suburbs of Philadelphia. He is also the founder of Kairos Partnerships, an initiative that trains, equips and partners with pastors and church planters through speaking, coaching and consulting in churches, parachurch organizations and nonprofits. He also serves as the Director of Leadership and Congregational Formation for The Ecclesia Network.

He is the creator of the Epic Fail Pastors' Conference, which helps pastors embrace failure and see it as an invitation to growth and an opportunity for grace and healing. He is the author of several books, including *Fail: Finding Hope and Grace in the Midst of Ministry Failure* (InterVarsity Press).

J.R. and his wife, Megan, have two sons, Carter and Bennett, and live in Lansdale, Pennsylvania.

www.jrbriggs.com
www.kairospartnerships.org
www.epicfailevents.com
www.twitter.com/jr_briggs

Bob Hyatt is the founding pastor of The Evergreen Community in Portland, Oregon. He has lived the church planter life and knows the stresses and joys inherent in it.

Coaching other pastors is a real joy for Bob as he helps pastors embrace the gospel and the formation that can come through ministry, knowing he is having an impact in many communities, for many people, most of whom he will never meet.

In addition to coaching and pastoring, Bob is the Director of Church and Movement Multiplication for the Ecclesia Network. He received his master's degree from Western Seminary in Portland and is currently pursuing a Doctor of Ministry in leadership and spiritual formation from George Fox Seminary.

In his off time, Bob loves reading and spending time with his wonderful family: his wife, Amy, and their children, Jack, Jane and Josie.

www.bobhyatt.me
www.twitter.com/bobhyatt